A
LIGHT
that is
SHINING
an introduction to the
Quakers

Second Edition

HARVEY GILLMAN

QUAKER HOME SERVICE
- London -

First edition published November 1988
reprinted 1991 and 1994.

This edition published February 1997
by

Quaker Home Service
Friends House, Euston Road, London NW1 2BJ.

© HARVEY GILLMAN 1997

ISBN 0-85245-287-X

PREFACE

This book is intended to introduce Quakers to people who, while they know little about them, would like to know more. Though it is my personal description of Quakers, I have tried to make it as objective as possible. The various drafts have been read by a number of Friends and a few friends who are not members of the Society. I am greatly indebted to them for their help and have tried to meet their points and adopt their suggestions wherever possible. This book is limited to the experience of Quakers in Britain and I have not attempted to write about those living in other parts of the world.

HARVEY GILLMAN

INTRODUCTION

CONTENTS

INTRODUCTION

I once found myself at dinner with a group of people I scarcely knew. Over soup the conversation turned to employment. I must admit I find it difficult discussing my job, Outreach Secretary to Quaker Home Service, because unlike being a teacher or a plumber, it means little to most people. I said 'I work for the Quakers'. Silence followed. Several eyes fell upon the soup in front of them, or looked through the window. Well, what do you say? 'How nice', or 'Oh dear, we shouldn't talk about religion' or 'They're good people, aren't they?', or 'Don't they spend a long time meditating in silence?', or the famous, 'Wasn't Elizabeth Fry something to do with them?' Often it is simply a conversation stopper. The host or hostess may well sigh and think that a substitute should have been found for the alcohol. 'You do drink orange juice, don't you?'

On that occasion, however, I was told that since it was not every day they had a Quaker to dinner, I was to earn my food by telling the gathering what Quakers were all about. It was quite a challenge and I do not know just how much they understood. I do remember that I was still talking as the ice-cream found its way onto my plate.

*I*n Britain there are about 18,000 members of the Religious Society of Friends, as Quakers are officially called. Around the world there are about 304,000 Quakers altogether, with large numbers in the United States, Latin America, and East Africa. Like most British Quakers I was not born into a Quaker family. I joined the Society in 1978 at the age of thirty. Five years later, I became Extension, now Outreach, Secretary of one of the departments based at Friends House, the central offices in London of Britain Yearly Meeting. My particular brief is to describe Quaker convictions and beliefs to enquirers who for a number of different reasons wish to know more about them. The difficulty is how to describe this strange and, to me, very attractive group of individuals who hold a variety of differing beliefs and who use a whole range of differing words to describe their experiences. This is the dilemma of this introductory book. I shall try to convey the range of convictions, ways of worshipping, consequences of religious insights in the area of social concern, and the somewhat odd structure, from a point that is both my own and yet, I hope, representative of the Society in Britain Yearly Meeting (that is England, Scotland and Wales) of which I am a member. It must be emphasised right from the beginning that for Quakers a general description of faith is likely to end up as the lowest common denominator of a number of differing points of view. So a personal statement may prove to be a way in to Quakerism rather than a barrier. At any rate I hope so.

A native American chief who once sat in the quiet of a Quaker meeting for worship said through an interpreter that he loved to hear 'where words come from'. He loved to listen to the silence beyond the words, to the inner meaning which words are often inadequate to express. I am conscious that words divide people, that one person's experience will lead to a rejection of words like 'God', or 'Christ', whereas another will feel that any reference to religious experience without them will be incomplete. Quakers believe that all people should listen to each other, to hear 'where words come from', to bear in mind that all human beings are on a journey, that we are all important, and that the attempts to describe what matters most to us are precisely the ones where we most often fail.

Religion and the Human Journey

The word 'religion' sets off an alarm bell in the minds of many people. It may smack of enforced hymn-singing at school, boring Sundays when you were not allowed to do things you especially wanted to. Or else it may remind you of people you know or have met, who spend their time being pious and telling other people how they should live their lives. On the other hand, it may summon up for you an area of life you know little about, as fewer and fewer families and schools pass their religious tradition to new generations. A recent survey for instance showed that many teenagers could say very little about the festival of Easter. Christmas, of course, is known more widely as for the most part it has become an annual binge, quite separate from the religious calendar.

For those of us who were born into a particular religious tradition, religion may evoke also the joys of childhood, the times when we were happy and secure and our parents had the answers and the world had meaning. If anyone then questions us about our faith, we may feel attacked and also suspect that the questioner is finding fault with our background and our family. We become defensive and say that religion is a topic you do not talk about in public. For all these reasons and because so much harm has been and is being done in the name of religion throughout the world, it is necessary to look at what we mean by religious experience. I want to start therefore not with an institution, or a book, or a series of rules, but with human experience, which is where Quakers usually begin.

The Human Journey

Elizabeth Kübler-Ross, a counsellor and writer, who specialises in work with the dying and the bereaved, has written:

> *Every individual human being born on this earth has the capacity to become a unique and special person unlike any who has ever existed before or will ever exist again.*[1]

It has been said that sex was the taboo subject of the nineteenth century. This is far from the case in our own century. Until a few years ago death was the taboo subject that had replaced it for us moderns. A society like ours which places so much emphasis on living life to the full, which often means the sheer pursuit of pleasure and possessions, obviously fears anything that stands in the way of this pursuit. Besides, we have put those close to death out of the way, into hospitals, hospices, and homes for the aged. Yet counsellors, psychologists and social workers are beginning to realise that we have to look at our fears of death, to help us live life more deeply.

Until recently religion was also becoming a taboo subject. Scientific progress had become a god and talk of spirituality, mysticism, 'the search for something deeper' was regarded, outside of certain prescribed areas, as decidedly cranky. This has changed in the last few years. More and more people are searching and are not afraid to admit it, though the results are not always positive and creative, as the proliferation of new and sometimes authoritarian cults reveals.

GEORGE FOX, bronze bust by Turner

A phrase much loved by Quakers and used frequently by George Fox (1624-1691), the great preacher of the early years, is that there is 'that of God' in everyone. I have pondered over the meaning of that phrase ever since I joined Quakers. In the next chapter, I shall look at it in greater depth, but it seems to me that it is something to do with a creative power working in our lives to bring us to fulfilment, to an awareness of our worth, to a love for others and for God. For a Quaker, religion is not an external activity, concerning a special 'holy' part of the self. It is an openness to the world in the here and now with the whole of the self. If this is not to be simply a pious commonplace, it must take into account the whole of our humanity: our attitudes to other human beings in our most intimate as well as social and political relationships. It must also take account of our life in the world around us, the way we live, the way we treat animals and the environment. In short, there is no part of ourselves and of our relationships where God is not present.

Each of us is unique. The test of any religious community is how far all its members are cherished as unique individuals with talents to contribute to the life of the community.

William Penn (1644-1718) was the founder of the once Quaker province of Pennsylvania in the now United States of America. His attempt to create a land of peace, harmony, and justice was a valiant effort to base a society on Quaker convictions. This attempt was called the 'Holy Experiment'. In a sense, I believe that the Religious Society of Friends is such an experiment. Like many experiments, things go wrong, people are hurt, reality does not always live up to the ideal. The attempt is made nevertheless to live out religion on a day to day basis and to respect the uniqueness and specialness of each person's experience. It is in this uniqueness that one can often see most clearly that power for love and creativity which is usually called God.

WILLIAM PENN AND THE INDIANS by Benjamin West

Friends House Library

Chapter One

THE FOUNDATION: *GOD WITHIN THE HEART*

*F*or much of their early history, Quakers suffered persecution, precisely for the courage they had in their everyday lives upholding their convictions. Even the name 'Quaker' was first used in contempt. When in 1650 George Fox appeared before a judge on charges of blasphemy, he told the judge that he should 'tremble at the word of the Lord'. The judge then described Fox and his followers as 'Quakers'. The name has stuck, but the other title 'Friends' (originally *Friends of the Truth*) is the one most often used amongst Quakers today. Besides, it is very pleasant in a group to refer to co-seekers and co-finders as *Friends*, even if they are strangers. It can create a good atmosphere for the building of community.

Quaker Convictions

You will not find the convictions of Quakers in this country set out in any creed. From early days they have stressed that their faith is something they live rather than put into particular words, and creeds can make simply for an outward conformity of belief. The formal creeds of the church as they have come down to us today were the results of the efforts of theologians to define what was true in opposition to the various 'heresies' current in several parts of Christendom. In this way orthodoxy (meaning right opinion) was established. Many who called themselves Christians were, through excommunication or even violence, cut off from the larger body for refusing to accept these verbal formulations of belief. The language in which the creeds were written was the language of the learned, often with the political support of the imperial authorities, so that many of the uneducated recited the creeds without understanding them.

I have already written that words are often divisive. The same word often means different things to different people and similar ideas are sometimes expressed in very dissimilar ways. So when it comes to talking about basic beliefs, Quakers have a certain mistrust of theological terminology.

As William Penn wrote:

> ...it is not opinion, or speculation, or notions of what is true, ... that ... makes a man a true believer, or a true Christian. But it is a conformity of mind and practice to the will of God, in all holiness of conversation (behaviour), according to the dictates of this divine principle of light and life in the soul. [2]

Early Quakers maintained that the church of New Testament times was composed of people who had a direct personal experience of what they described as God's saving power, and who acted out their lives accordingly. For these early Christians what mattered was experience not intellectual assent to doctrines. The Quaker pioneers believed that personal religious faith was of the same nature. They claimed that they were reviving primitive Christianity and that they too like their spiritual forebears were the children of God. They felt however that the other churches of their day had lost the spontaneous experience of God beneath age-old accretions of institutionalism, non-Biblical doctrines, and violent oppression of one group by another.

What then is the foundation of the Religious Society of Friends? I should put it this way: there is a creative, loving power in all people and in the world around. Many call it God, though it is beyond all names. Everyone can become aware of it directly by listening to its promptings in their hearts and in the hearts of others.

Quakers feel more able to become aware of this power in the silence of their meetings for worship. In the quiet, they maintain, the still, small voice can speak to them and direct their lives. The experience of quiet waiting upon God gives them strength to go back into the bustle of the world, the better to serve their fellows.

It is not through religious institutions, or in the hallowed pages of a book, that God is most keenly to be found, but in the human heart. For most Quakers, the model of this meeting with the divine and its transforming power in everyday life is Jesus of Nazareth, his life, his teaching, and his death and its empowering effect on others. The rest of this book is really a commentary on these convictions.

As human beings, we can find fulfilment in our relationship with this power, whatever name we give to it. It gives meaning and purpose to our lives. It is our focus of unity. That it touches all parts of human existence leads Quakers to assert that life cannot be separated into categories of 'sacred' and 'secular'. Nor can we divide the world into compartments labelled 'religious', 'political', 'social' and so on. The way we act in every sphere depends greatly on what we believe about the nature of the world. John Woolman (1720-1772), an American Quaker whose profound religious convictions led him to the campaign to abolish slavery and to a compassionate concern for animals, saw the interconnectedness of all life and wrote in his journal:

> to say we love God...and at the same time exercise
> cruelty toward the least creature moving by his life,

or by life derived from him, was a contradiction in itself.

So the Quaker faith is a holistic one, taking all experience as its arena.

This openness to what Quakers call 'the leadings of the Spirit' is seen most evidently in the way Quakers worship, as will be described in the next chapter. Because Quakers believe that there is 'that of God' in everyone they have no special ordained ministry. They recognise that each worshipper has particular gifts and that all present have an important part to play. This has led to a belief in the equality of the sexes and within their meetings for worship women play an equal part with men. Although Quakers have always been influenced by contemporary prejudices, they have nevertheless made a progressive and positive impact in the field of women's rights.

The Light within the Darkness

When trying to communicate the truths that you have discovered through your own experience, it is often easier to talk in images than to resort to intellectual theories. Jesus himself taught through parables which were images from the everyday experience of his listeners. He spoke of the seed and the lamp, the treasure and the sparrow. When in the seventeenth century Quakers studied The Bible they noticed how few of the big words of theology were ever used there. There is no mention there for example of the words 'trinity' or 'sacrament'. So, because they thought themselves to be direct inheritors of the early church, they refused to use these words to define their beliefs. However, one of the key words Quakers have always used is the word 'light', which they associated with the risen Christ in their hearts.

Light is a natural and beautiful image even in these days of neon and the hologram. It represents security, warmth, and knowledge. It also however has an opposite side. It is no friend to that part of ourselves we should like to keep hidden. We do not always want all our faults to be brought forth into the light of day. It would be false to human experience so to emphasise the light that we neglected the darkness.

In his journal, George Fox wrote of his own unhappy youth as being a struggle against depression and melancholia and a fervent longing for God. In a passage dated 1647 he spoke of his inward sufferings and his inability to understand why he had to undergo 'great temptations'. He wrote:

> And I cried to the Lord, saying 'why should I be thus, seeing I was never addicted to commit those evils?' And the Lord answered that it was needful I should have a sense of all conditions, how else should I speak to all conditions; and in this I saw the infinite love of God. I saw also that there was an ocean of darkness and death, but an infinite ocean of light and love, which flowed over the ocean of darkness.[3]

This passage, often quoted by modern Quakers, points not to an empty optimism about the world, as if to say 'God is in his heaven. All's right with the world.' On the contrary, Fox, like other Christians, believed that suffering is part of the world's process, but that there is something greater than even the greatest suffering. There is a light which as John's Gospel has it (in the *New English Bible* version) 'shines on in the dark, and the darkness has never mastered it' and that light 'enlightens every man' (and woman).

Suffering

You are unlikely to come across the view among Quakers that there is a God in a heaven beyond death whose philosophy is 'a good dose of punishment never did anyone any harm and often does a lot of good'. Yet obviously suffering does exist. It is wrong to talk of suffering as always ennobling its victims and it does a great disservice to many who have suffered much to try to explain away its presence. The world is full of innocent victims and talk of sin as the cause of suffering has often in the past simply been a means of oppressing the powerless and keeping them in their place.

In his book *Night*, Elie Wiesel, the modern Jewish writer and Nobel Prize winner, wrote of his experiences of Auschwitz and Buchenwald. There is one particularly harrowing incident which remains with me. Wiesel describes the death of a young boy in Auschwitz. A power station had been blown up by anti-Nazi saboteurs and the boy was to be executed for refusing to name the perpetrators. The inmates were assembled to watch the boy and two other prisoners die. Their necks were placed in nooses. The two adults to be murdered shouted 'Long live liberty!' Someone standing behind the author asked 'Where is God? Where is He?' The three victims were then hanged. The inmates had to watch the boy dying for more than half an hour.

Wiesel writes:

> Behind me, I heard the same man asking:
> 'Where is God now?'

> And I heard a voice within me answer him:
> 'Where is He?
> Here He is - He is hanging on this gallows...' [4]

I have often meditated on this incident. It has come to me while sitting in the silence of a meeting for worship as the ultimate question. The words are so ambiguous. Does Wiesel mean that his idea of God died the moment the boy died? In his novel *La Peste* (*The Plague*), Albert Camus likewise described the death of an innocent boy, this time through the plague. His conclusion was that he could not accept a God in a world where the innocent suffer. But Wiesel is much more ambiguous. As I re-read the first passage and meditate on it, my faith leads me to believe in a God who suffers with the world, and is crucified and resurrected, as it were, in the thousand moments of our pains and joys. The question then is not so much why suffering exists. Multitudes of books have been written on that theme and they have persuaded very few people. The question is: What do we do with suffering? George Fox in the passage from his journal has the telling phrase, 'I should have a sense of all conditions'. It is the wounded healer, the one who accepts the wounds, not passively but with a view to using them actively as a source of growth, and going out to help others with their wounds, that seems to me to be the model for the person of faith today. And it is not meant to be easy.

The Search

Quakers do not spend much time talking about sin. They tend to emphasise the good in people. The feeling of a lack of self-worth is strong enough in most people without 'preaching up sin' as early Quakers put it. But when we read many of the early journals (and it was the custom of Quakers to write journals instead of books of theology - personal experience over intellectual theories again), we can see a process of overcoming this sense of low self-worth. There is at first a feeling of inauthenticity, of life not lived fully or honestly; then there is a flicker of an insight that life does have meaning. Sometimes this may come in a blinding flash, at other times as a result of a long period of perplexity.

The period of inauthenticity, of dullness, of alienation, might be described as a period of sin or the dark night of the soul. But then gradually the individual feels that there is a power working within which says 'No, you can't go on like this. Something has to change'. This is accompanied by an almost physical apprehension, a quaking even, or a nagging feeling that you have to take up your tent and move on. This struggle is in most of us a continuous one. At times we feel we have come through, made it to the light; at other times we feel, here we go again into the darkness. Isaac Penington (1616-1679) was a man who went from sect to sect, always discontented with what he found in each group. At last he became a Quaker. In his journal he writes:

> And indeed, at last, when my nature was almost spent, and the pit of despair was even closing its mouth upon me, mercy sprang, and deliverance came, and the Lord my God owned me, and sealed his love unto me, and light sprang within me.[5]

Even when he became a Quaker, there must have been moments when doubt took over again; and yet doubts and perplexities can be creative, for they also have a positive role to play in spiritual development.

The Directness of the Experience
Quakers do not believe this journey of spiritual growth is for a few exceptional people. It is one which all people are making at all times and in all places. As has already been mentioned, Quakers do not make a distinction between

the sacred and the secular. This does not devalue the sacred but upgrades the secular.

Quakers share with other mystics the insight that God can be found in the everyday experience of all people. It is in the here and now that communion, real sharing, can occur. I have in the past stayed for short periods in monasteries for the quiet and peacefulness of the surroundings. I have noticed more and more that if we think that we can escape from the world's problems by taking on a 'holy' life we are often much mistaken. The world is always with us even in the most set aside places. This is one of the deep insights of monastic life. One monastic tradition which I find very appealing is the law of hospitality: each guest is Christ at the door waiting to come in. At this point the Catholic and the Quaker traditions are very close, for the holy is part of ordinary experience, the guest and Christ are one, when seen with the eyes of faith and compassion.

Just as Quakers do not limit the service of God to certain times, or places, or people, so they do not have a set apart priesthood, nor a religious calendar of events. Nor do they have set hymns, and the meeting houses in which they worship are not consecrated. They do not have set sacraments such as water baptism and literal breaking of the bread. Following the Protestant move away from the hierarchical church of pre-Reformation Europe, Quakers took the idea of the priesthood of all believers to its extreme. According to Lewis Benson, the modern American student of George Fox, in his *George Fox's Message is Relevant Today*, Quakers taught:

> *As he (Christ) teaches he can be known as prophet.*
> *As he forgives and intercedes he is known as priest...*
> *As he guides and watches over us he is known as*

shepherd. He can also be known as counsellor and leader and commander.[6]

If that is the case then there is no need for any specific person to be designated prophet, priest, or church leader. Quakers would say that if people are open to the power of love and light in their lives then they will themselves become prophetic and priestly, and will not need to follow the external authority of church leaders. They will become empowered to find God in their hearts and to serve other people.

Quakers and Christianity

No water baptism, no priests, no creeds, no religious festivals, just how Christian then are Quakers? Quakers in Britain and Ireland are members of the Council of Churches for Britain and Ireland. Most Churches are members through the acceptance of a creed, but Quakers, not having a creed, are admitted by member churches under a special clause. So we are seen to be Christian by other churches. The problem is of course one of meaning. According to a conservative evangelical definition, if you do not accept The Bible as literally the true word of God, or do not have faith in the redemption and atonement by Christ on the cross, then you are not a Christian. This would exclude from the Christian community many people, even in the more mainstream churches.

In his great work on Quakerism known as the *Apology*, Robert Barclay (1648-1690), a Scottish aristocrat and Quaker theologian, wrote of the church as a body consisting of those who were:

obedient of the holy light and testimony of God in their hearts... There may be members therefore of this Catholic church both among heathens, Turks,

*Jews, and all the several sorts of Christians, men
and women of integrity, and simplicity of heart.*[7]

This definition is much more universal in its application
than the conservative definition and is based on a meeting
with God in the heart, a turning to the light within. However
Quakers define Christianity, and there are differences
among them, they see it as making for an open, inclusive
community. There are a few who prefer not to use Christian
language at all and even maintain that they are Quaker,
not Christian. Certainly very few Quakers in Britain today
would accept the conservative evangelical view. Most would
say that for them the teachings and life of Jesus of Nazareth
were central to the picture they have of God. For some
Jesus is God in a trinitarian sense; for others he is the
supreme ethical teacher; for yet others he is the human
being who has reached his divine potential.

My own position is that all human beings have this
potential and that Jesus of Nazareth through his life, his
teaching, his death, shows me the way to God; but the
more I read The Bible the more I am convinced that Jesus
the Jew did not aim to begin a new religion. He seems to
have wanted to liberate human beings, to enable them to
have a more personal and dynamic relationship with God.
In doing this he points back to Old Testament prophets
like Isaiah. At the same time he seems to have realised
that the path he was taking could be seen in terms of the
suffering servant which Isaiah himself describes. The
suffering servant accepts upon his shoulders the pain of
the world even to his own death.

Modern Biblical scholarship also tends to stress that
what was described by the early church is not so much the
actual life of Jesus as much as the church's own
interpretation of it during the years after the crucifixion.

• The New Testament is the recorded experience of those close to Jesus. Quakers believe the spirit that inspired the early church is still alive today and that spirit is not bound to any one religious tradition. Indeed when Barclay was describing the 'catholic church' (that is, the church universal) he also mentioned that it included

> all ...of whatsoever nations, kindred, tongue or people, they be, though outwardly strangers and remote from those who profess Christ and Christianity in words.[8]

It is not the word or the labels but the heart and the commitment beneath them that counts.

Many of the early opponents of Friends claimed that the Quakers denied Christ, The Bible, even God. To me, however, it seems that they were expanding the experience of God to include 'that of God in everyone', a sort of universalist Christianity.

Guidelines

A good introduction to the breadth of British Quaker experience and conviction is *Quaker Faith & Practice - the book of Christian discipline of the Yearly Meeting of the Religious Society of Friends (Quakers) in Britain*. The subtitle sounds formidable. 'Discipline' here has a particular sense, it refers to a common purpose and conviction. 'Discipleship' might be a more accurate word.

The book is an anthology of writings from the earliest days of the Society to the present day. It is revised each generation in accordance with the Quaker belief in continuing revelation. Our understanding of truth is not static: new light is always being sought and often it is found.

The book opens with *Advices and Queries*, a series of questions and insights in English and Welsh, which are used both for personal reflection and for reading aloud during meeting for worship. The first advice provides a good introduction to Quaker thought:

> *Take heed, dear Friends, to the promptings of love and truth in your hearts. Trust them as the leadings of God whose Light shows us our darkness and brings us to new life.*[9]

Among the matters dealt with in this book are approaches to God, worship, structure, ways of conducting business, living faithfully today, close relationships, social responsibility, the peace testimony and the unity of creation. It is a work of inspiration, a masterpiece of the spiritual search.

Chapter Two

WORSHIP: *A QUIET WAITING*

*O*n *one never-to-be-forgotten Sunday morning, I found myself one of a small company of silent worshippers who were content to sit together without words, that each one might feel after and draw near to the Divine Presence, unhindered at least, if not helped, by any human utterance. Utterance I knew was free, should the words be given; and before the meeting was over, a sentence or two were uttered in great simplicity by an old and apparently untaught man, rising in his place amongst the rest of us. I did not pay much attention to the words he spoke and I have no recollection of their purport. My whole soul was filled with the unutterable peace of the undisturbed opportunity for communion with God, with the sense that at last I have found a place where I might, without the faintest suspicion of insincerity, join with others in simply seeking His presence. To sit in silence could at least pledge me to nothing; it might open to me (as it did that morning) the very gate of heaven.*[10]

This passage written almost one hundred years ago by Caroline Stephen, the aunt of the novelist Virginia Woolf, reflects the experience of many people when they attend their first Quaker meeting for worship. Many find it an experience like that of coming home after a long journey. Of course, it does not always work this way. Some people get little out of it, some are bored, others find it a peaceful, pleasant time but would not go further than that. Quakers have learned to be rather fearful of too strong emotions in worship which in the past have proved divisive and it would not be expected that a meeting for worship should leave the worshipper ecstatic. It could better be described as a quiet waiting on God. But there are moments like those Caroline Stephen described, when the worshippers may feel deeply and spiritually moved by an awareness of the divine. It can be a life transforming experience.

One of the problems is the word 'worship' itself. It can sound as if one were bowing and scraping before some tyrannical master. In fact the word derives from the word 'worth'. It is the time Quakers give to finding worth in their lives. Here there are no hymns, no sermons, no set prayers. There is an hour of stillness, of inward prayer, contemplation, and reflection. Anyone who feels moved to do so, may speak out of his or her experience: this is called vocal ministry. Ministry in this sense is not a function of an individual but a gift that all may exercise. At the end of the hour, the worshippers shake hands and the meeting is over.

photo Andrew Backhouse

MEETING FOR WORSHIP

To someone looking in from the outside, nothing may appear to be happening. For the participant, however, it is a contemplative and meditative experience, and above all a corporate activity. Meditation, especially as practised by some eastern religions, can be an escape from consciousness, an emptying of the self. At its best a Quaker meeting for worship is a fullness. The worshippers are filled with a deep feeling of the Presence among them. This may sometimes lead them to an assurance that, to use Mother Julian of Norwich's words, 'all will be well' (and this in spite of the difficulties and problems besetting the world around). Whereas in some eastern meditation, the devotee is led away from the world, in the Quaker meeting, one is led back - it has been said, 'When worship ends, service begins'. Through worship the individual becomes part of a large community of worshippers who are friends in the widest sense.

The meeting for worship is a public event, to which anyone is welcome. In meeting everyone has a part to play; the visitor is welcomed, the regular attender is cherished, the member feels at home. Within the meeting for worship itself no distinction is made, all are part of the quiet waiting, all are free to speak or remain silent.

Silence is precious and healing. As Caroline Stephen put it, 'To sit down in silence could at least pledge me to nothing'. One does not lose by undertaking the experience. On the contrary, in a civilisation like ours where little value is given to silence and to listening, a Quaker meeting can be very therapeutic. At one meeting I attended, an elderly woman used to fall asleep each Sunday. Far from being put out by this, the local Quakers told me that she found it very difficult to sleep at home and the meeting for worship was the only occasion when she could sleep properly. They were delighted that they had provided the opportunity for her to fall into a healing sleep.

A Visit to Meeting

The word 'meeting' needs some explanation. Firstly, a meeting is a place, as in 'Swansea Meeting'. Secondly it is the collective noun for the worshippers at a certain place as in 'Westminster Meeting has decided to redecorate its kitchens'. Thirdly, it is the occasion at which the group meets for worship - in this case it is short for 'meeting for worship'. Quakers say 'I am going to meeting this morning' as other Christians would say 'I am going to church'.

Because Quakers are quite small in numbers and meeting houses are scattered it is often difficult to find them. If you had looked in the phone book you may have had to look for Friends, or Society of Friends, or Religious Society of Friends, or Quakers, and then you would not necessarily know who you were talking to. It could be the warden of the meeting house, or the resident Friend, or caretaker, the clerk, an elder, or an overseer (we will consider these terms later). So if you have succeeded in speaking to a Quaker or finding a meeting house, you have performed no mean feat. This is not because they are trying to remain invisible, but because there are often so few Quakers or the meeting house is out of the way. Some local groups of Quakers may not be as publicity conscious as they might be and this can make finding them more difficult.

So you have found the meeting house. Or it might be a room in a community centre, school, church hall or a private house. The building itself may be three hundred years old or brand new, but whatever its age, it will be simple and functional. When you go in, you may well be greeted at the

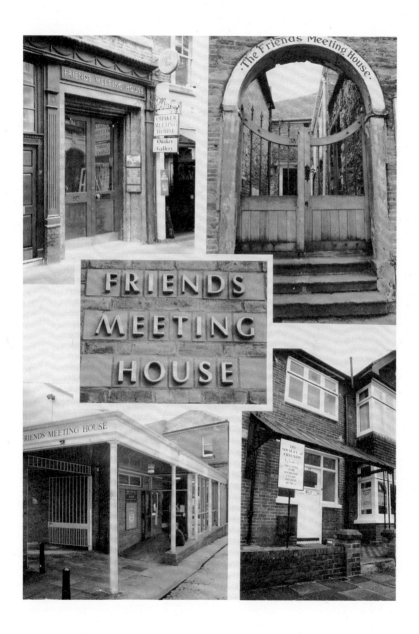

door with a friendly handshake. You will find inside no religious symbolism: no statues, no crosses, no crucifix, no altar, no pulpit. In the entrance hall you may find people waiting to go in, reading pamphlets, studying lists of activities, handing each other notices to be read out after meeting has ended, or just chatting. Most meeting houses have libraries and pamphlet racks and you will be most welcome to take any leaflet that interests you. In some Meetings, if you are new, the Friend who greets you at the door of the meeting room may hand you a leaflet called *Your First Time in a Quaker Meeting?* You may be grateful for this during the next hour, as an hour of silence may be a new experience for you and it is good to have something to read or hold to help you settle down.

The meeting for worship begins when the first person sits down in the silence. One advice beloved of Quakers from the *Advices and Queries* is 'Come faithfully to meeting for worship with heart and mind prepared'. This does not mean preparing a speech in advance. That would spoil the spontaneity of the worship. What it does mean is keeping meeting for worship and your fellow worshippers in your mind during the week so that the weekly meeting is not an addition to or a substitute for your prayer life, but an integral part of it. Some Quakers try to set apart a short period each day for silent contemplation as it is difficult trying to pack the whole of one's week's worship into one hour on Sunday morning. Coming with heart and mind prepared also means arriving on a Sunday in a relaxed state so that you can enter into the worship without difficulty. This is not always easy of course, if you have to see to the children, prepare the meal, or cover some distance to get to meeting. This intermingling of silence and daily life is found also in the silence before meals that many Quakers observe. The whole of life and all its activities become a sort of communion.

So into the meeting room. You will find a simple room with chairs or benches arranged in a square or a circle. In the centre is a table with a vase and flowers and usually copies of The Bible and *Quaker Faith & Practice*. You will see the worshippers in all sorts of postures, thoughtful, meditative, worried, looking out of the window, stroking their beards or clasping their beads, eyes closed, eyes open, all of them seated. Some may have adopted the hands-open-facing-upwards-on-the-knees posture which derives both from Buddhism and medieval Christian mysticism and is also used by some Christian charismatics. Whatever posture is natural to you is the one to adopt. Righteousness does not come from a bruised bottom or a strained shoulder.

When I go to meeting on Sunday I have a particular pattern that I sometimes follow. I sit down and watch the other people coming into the room. I often greet them with a smile or a slight nod of the head. After all, it is a society of friends and it is good actually to greet your friends when you see them. I then recite quietly to myself the 'Lord's Prayer' taking each phrase slowly, almost like a Buddhist mantra. I close my eyes and thoughts rise up from my life which demand my attention.

On Prayer and Distraction

During the rest of the hour anything may happen. I may 'hold in the light' people who are going through a difficult time. I may even get to a point of stillness where I feel one with the world and then I do not need words or thoughts at all. I may follow the words spoken by others and be led into an area I had not anticipated at all. I may be inspired by the sound of a bird outside or led into a voyage of inner discovery through the passing of an aeroplane overhead. It is not knowing which so appeals to me. The fact that I may be touched by the moment, touched into joy, sadness, even despair or radiance - all gifts of the Spirit. I am sometimes touched by nothing at all, enfolded in doubt or uncertainty. These are also necessary stages of vulnerability. Then the meeting will end as two appointed Friends, the elders, shake hands which is usually followed nowadays by a general shaking of hands by everyone present.

Once I took part in a series of Ignatian exercises led by an Anglican priest. These exercises take their name from Ignatius of Loyola, founder of the Roman Catholic Society of Jesus (Jesuits). During these exercises, we were told that thoughts often arise in a silence because we have been so busy during our week that we have repressed certain things which now leap up to demand consideration. It may be, it was suggested, that we had to pay some attention to these thoughts and our worship was precisely the time we could deal with them. The Quaker meeting for worship is not a time just for holy reflections and for chasing away the lower breeds of thought. In fact the more you try to push away thoughts you do not want to think about, the more they persist. Thomas Merton, the great twentieth-century Trappist monk and writer, wrote that thoughts were like birds. You could let them fly around your head, but you need not let them build their nests there. So if a distracting thought arises during meeting for worship, let it be for a short time. We all have troubled thoughts at times; we are not saints, just seekers.

Prayer

One of the questions which often worries newcomers and established Quakers alike is that of prayer. What is prayer and what do we do when we pray?

Isaac Penington described prayer as the 'breathing of the child to the Father which begat it'. It may be described as a human response to the world around; an awareness of ourselves, of others, of that power most of us call God, working in the world, loving it, transforming it, and empowering us. The problem is that we often think of prayers in the plural rather than prayer in general. Prayers seem to be formulas, words we recite; prayer on the contrary is a state of awareness where not even words may be necessary.

I once met a Benedictine monk who was interested in the Religious Society of Friends. His problem was that he was tired of the repetition of words. There is a Catholic form of spirituality which believes that prayer is like a boat and that we can sail upon the words, even when we feel we should prefer to remain in port. The words help us along. There is good insight in this. But there are times when weariness takes over. This monk and I agreed that it would be nice if there could be a sort of silent mass. After all, what are the ingredients of the mass? There is a general preparation and awareness of our shortcomings (confession), prayers to the glory of God, ministry of the word, the creed, prayers on behalf of the world and the people, sharing of the peace, the preparation of gifts and thanksgiving for them, prayers of consecration, communion, thanksgiving for communion, and the dismissal.

Yet, however formal all these may appear, they have their counterpart in everyday life. We prepare ourselves for meeting, aware of how we have not lived up to our ideals during the week. We open ourselves up to the world of creation, often with no more than a 'thank you', just as in confession we may have been able to utter no more than 'I'm sorry, I've done it again'. We bring to mind the needs of our friends, problems in the world, we think of people who have meant much to us. Thinking lovingly is a form of prayer. Of course Quakers do not recite creeds, even silent ones, but they are mindful of their basic convictions, their place in the world, and how the world might be made more holy by their actions and their love.

Ministry

The word 'ministry' is often heard among Quakers in a much broader sense than elsewhere. Ministry is service. Quakers form a community in which they each serve each other in a number of different ways. There is no hierarchy of ministry; no one function is holier than another. The Friend who stands at the door performs the service of welcoming the worshipper to the worship. For some people, especially newcomers or those who live alone and have lost or never had the intimacy of touch, this is a very important ministry. It can be an affirmation of their presence at a level much beyond that of words. There is the ministry of the one who has arranged the flowers on the centre table, a task often regarded as a humble one, but in fact these flowers may take on in the worship a symbolism of growth and new life. They are a witness to creation.

And there is the ministry of the word, when the worshipper is moved to stand up and to speak from his or her experience. This vocal ministry may take the form of a prayer, a Bible reading, a reading from other literature, or more commonly may arise from the experience of the speaker. The meeting for worship is a public event and the speaker need not be a member. It is the Spirit that is speaking through the words of the person who ministers, and the words are shared by everyone. Sometimes the meeting may be completely silent for an hour. It is not only the action or the word that counts - simply being there as a sharer is a service in itself.

The impulse to minister often seems to force itself upon the speaker and this may be accompanied by a quickening of the pulse. Indeed early Quakers were known for their trembling before God, but on the whole Quaker ministry today seems to be characterised more by its intensity than by outward signs of emotion though I have heard ministry forced out of speakers through their tears. The sincerity that shines through shows that ministry has come from a deep place in the life of the speaker. This ministry does not interrupt the silence but acts as a sort of vocal counterpart or counterpoint. Thomas Kelly (1893-1941) was an American Quaker whose writings on spirituality have made an impact beyond the Quaker family. In his *The Gathered Meeting*, he wrote:

> *Brevity, earnestness, sincerity - and frequently a lack of polish - characterize the best Quaker speaking. The words should rise like a shaggy crag upthrust from the surface of the silence, under the pressure of river power and yearning, contrition and wonder ... They should not break the silence, but continue it.*[11]

At times what is said in meeting may not seem to fit in with your personal thoughts or may even sound contradictory. The feeling in a Quaker meeting is such that you may even be able to accept the ministry of others without agreeing on an intellectual level. Loving another person does not always mean accepting fully what he or she is saying. Above all, a Quaker meeting is not a debating chamber. It is not a matter of simply exchanging ideas about the world, however profound these ideas may be. It is a focussing of concern about the world at a deeper level, an affirmation of relationship and community, and a reaching out towards that which is both beyond and within. Though the worshipper may come to meeting tired, peevish, reluctant (and sometimes even leave in a similar mood), worship is a declaration like that of the boy Samuel in the temple: 'Speak, for I am listening'.

Meeting for Worship usually takes place on a Sunday but there is no Quaker religious calendar. Early Friends' rejection of Christmas and Easter as set times of the year was for them an affirmation of the ever present birth, death, and resurrection of Christ in their hearts. Indeed many Quakers used to keep their shops open on established religious festivals as a witness to this fact. In the eyes of others however this was sometimes seen as a canny way of earning more money! Nowadays, although this remains the Quaker position, some Quaker Meetings do hold a meeting for worship on Christmas day and also have carol singing. Easter likewise is often a time of special reflection on the theme of death and resurrection.

So strong was the reluctance to accept a church calendar that one early group of Friends even refused to believe that one ought to plan meetings for worship at all. The practical side of Quakerism is very strong, however. Most Quakers worship on a Sunday morning (set time) in a meeting house (set place) but this is for reasons of convenience, not because Sunday is a holier day than the rest of the week. As public transport in some areas gets steadily worse, some groups may well find that Sunday is an impossible day to meet and they may choose another day.

Children and Young People in Meeting

Children and young people are important members of the family of the Meeting. Some Meetings have many children and young people at different ages and different levels of development. In these Meetings there may be two, three or even four groups meeting in various parts of the meeting house or even in the homes of worshippers. There are also a few elderly Meetings where younger people are rarely if ever seen, though it is in these places that the worshippers are particularly delighted to see them.

Many of the very young would have difficulty in remaining for an hour in the silence of the meeting for worship though some appreciate it. It is usual for children to stay in meeting for the first ten or fifteen minutes or to come in towards the end. During their absence, they may be discussing Bible stories or Quaker traditions, using crafts, games and other activities to develop their own understanding and insights. They may also be weaving, helping to prepare the tea or coffee that are offered to all the worshippers at the end of meetings, or singing songs from *The Quaker Songbook*. The aim of the children's or young people's group is to give its members an awareness of being part of the community, a knowledge of its spiritual traditions, and of having a positive role in the larger community around them. At one Meeting I visited not long ago, the children were learning to bake bread and to understand its importance in the life of many different societies. It was an introduction to problems of famine, to Biblical symbolism, as well as being an enjoyable activity in itself.

In spite of their traditional reputation for dourness, Quakers actually like enjoying themselves, and of course teaching is best accomplished through fun. They do not indoctrinate their children but try to communicate something of the joy that they themselves have found in their life together. In one Meeting, the children put on a play about the life of Martin Luther King after worship one Sunday morning. It was very well performed and had been written by a member of the Meeting. It was a privilege to realise that we were all learning through this performance, learning of the life of the great black American leader, learning of the sufferings of the African Americans, learning of how suffering could be overcome. We ended up by singing 'We Shall Overcome'. We realised that we had been led in an act of worship by our children through joy and song.

Some older children prefer to stay in meeting with their parents and sometimes take part themselves in vocal ministry. At Young Friends' gatherings there are often experiments with different forms of worship, some silent, some more programmed and including music. It would be a mistake to presume that silence only appeals to older age ranges; a number of young people have been drawn to the Society through the stillness of its worship.

It is always advisable to check with Meetings to find out what facilities are offered for younger people, as sometimes there are meetings for them once or twice a month only. At other Meetings there may be no official arrangements made for younger age ranges, but Friends there would be very pleased to arrange sessions for them.

Weddings

It may seem odd to include Quaker weddings in a chapter on worship, but the marriage ceremony among Quakers follows the same lines as the usual meeting for worship. It is a specially appointed meeting yet the Quaker hallmarks of simplicity, openness, and spontaneity are all present. The ceremony begins in silence. Towards the beginning of the meeting a Friend will stand to explain to newcomers and family guests the procedure which will follow. The bride and bridegroom stand when they feel ready, take each other by the hand and make their declarations. First one partner speaks: *'Friends, I take this friend* (full name) *to be my wife/husband, promising, through divine assistance* (or 'with

CERTIFICATE OF MARRIAGE

(TO BE USED ONLY FOR MARRIAGES CONDUCTED IN ACCORDANCE WITH THE REGULATIONS
OF THE CHRISTIAN DISCIPLINE OF THE RELIGIOUS SOCIETY OF FRIENDS IN GREAT BRITAIN)

Roger John Holloway,
of 35 Lawrence Road, Southsea,
and Susan Stoppani
of the same address,

having made known their intention of taking each other in marriage and public
notice of their intention having been given, the proceedings were allowed
by the proper officers of *Southampton* and *Portsmouth*
Monthly Meeting of the Religious Society of Friends.
This is to certify that for the solemnisation of their marriage, *Roger John Holloway*
and *Susan Stoppani* were present at a duly appointed public meeting
for worship of the Society at *Portsmouth* this *twenty first*
day of *September* nineteen hundred and *ninety one*.
Taking each other by the hand,
Roger John Holloway declared:
Friends, I take this my Friend Susan Stoppani to be my wife,
promising with God's help, to be unto her a loving and faithful husband,
so long as we both on earth shall live.
and *Susan Stoppani* declared:
Friends, I take this my Friend Roger John Holloway to be my husband
promising with God's help, to be unto him a loving and faithful wife,
so long as we both on earth shall live.
In confirmation of these declarations they have in this meeting signed this
certificate of marriage.

Susan Stoppani

Roger Holloway
Edward Holloway
D. N. Holloway.

WE *having been present at the above marriage have also subscribed*
our names *as witnesses the day and year above written*

Philip Wilkins.

Janette Stoppani

Dorothy Morton.

Mary Furlong	*Jeanne Adams*	*Ben Read.*	*Megan Keys*
A. John Archer	*Robin Evelyn*	*Megan Lewis*	*Robert Keys.*
Graham Shipway	*Deirdre Milne*	*Karen Brown*	*Oliver Reid*
Carolynn Shipway	*Sarah Cople*	*Helen B W 16*	*Rosemary Simpson*
B J Shipway	*Andy Clarke*	*Marjorie Holloway*	*Susan Li*
Jane Lewis	*Desmond Green*	*Ann Leonard*	*Kay Cotton*
Wendy Wood	*Freda Green*	*Rachel Bone*	*Dorothy Taylor.*
Joe Carr	*John Holland*	*S. H. Bow*	*Daniel Read*
Myra Dale	*Saubreta Band*	*Anna Duncan.*	*Dorothy A. Richardson*
	Harry Oley.	*Molly*	*Ray Furlong*
Ennis Lewis	*Peter Otley.*	*Richard Read*	
Bernard Moss.	*John Adams.*	*Sally Read*	
		NORA ALDER,	

41

God's help') to be unto her/him a loving and faithful wife/ husband, so long as we both on earth shall live'. The other partner then makes a similar declaration. When the declarations have been made, the meeting continues with a period of silence. As in a usual meeting for worship, vocal prayer or ministry relating to the people being married, may arise out of the silence.

After this, the couple sign the marriage certificate which is then witnessed by all those present. Later the Registering Officer, appointed by the local Monthly Meeting, reads the certificate. The couple also sign the Civil Register. Traditionally Quakers did not wear wedding rings but nowadays couples often choose to exchange rings. An increasing number of Quaker women retain their own family names as a sign of equality between the sexes.

Sometimes the Quaker marriage procedure is used by people who are not Quakers. The decision to allow this is made by the Monthly Meeting. Usually one or both of the partners will have some association with Quakers and will be in sympathy with Quaker ideals. In this case also, the meeting for worship is a public event.

Funerals and Memorial Meetings

Quakers do not have a corporate 'line' on life after death. If you take experience as the basis for knowledge, then few Quakers have had a return ticket to the beyond to describe what they have found! The range of views vary from a personal survival after death, through an impersonal 'all will be one', to views which border on 'I don't really believe there is anything, but I know love must continue in some way or another'. The emphasis is always on living life fully in the here and now, and leaving the rest to God. Ideas of eternal punishment and damnation have little part to play in Quaker thinking. Nor is the hope of life after death seen simply as a reward for virtue, or as a reward for a difficult life. So at a funeral or at a later memorial meeting, in thinking of someone who has just died, Quakers concentrate lovingly on the life of the late Friend.

The meeting for worship on this occasion has no set form apart from the usual meeting. It may be held at a graveside, the crematorium, or in the meeting house. It is a service of thanksgiving for the grace of God displayed in the life of the departed, with thoughts of comfort and sympathy for those left behind. For this reason, Quakers tend not to wear black; even in death, however much the mourners grieve, it is for the gift of life and God's love that thanks be given. Thus these meetings, though serious, are not necessarily solemn and can often reach a great depth. For some people, they are their first experience of Quaker worship and at least one Friend now maintains that he joined the Society because of the way Quakers conducted their funerals.

All this refers to meetings in Britain, mainland Europe and in various parts of the United States, Canada, Australia, New Zealand and Southern Africa. In other parts of the States, South America and Africa you may meet 'programmed' Friends. The worship here tends to be prearranged with prayers and hymns. It may well be led by a pastor. Even here there will be spontaneous parts to the worship and sometimes periods of silence.

Chapter Three

ORIGINS AND DEVELOPMENT:
THE GROWTH OF THE QUAKER OUTLOOK

*T*his chapter needs only to be brief as there are several books published on Quaker history, perhaps the best recent one being John Punshon's *Portrait in Grey*. I have always found history fascinating but mainly for the parallels it draws with the present situation. Early Quakers saw their movement as 'primitive Christianity revived': they saw a parallel between their own seventeenth century and the first century when the church was expanding from Jerusalem outwards throughout the Roman Empire. Twentieth-century British Quakers have become more and more interested in their seventeenth-century origins as they have learnt to distance themselves a little from the more narrow evangelical Quakerism of the nineteenth century.

What we at this period of our history find striking about early Quakers in the 1640's and 50's is their emergence at a time of revolutionary change which was breaking down old ideas of a strictly defined social order. The Roman Catholic church had long ceased to have any power in Britain, although it was still feared by the political establishment. There was conflict in the Church of England between its Puritan and Catholic wings. There was a questioning about the role of the bishops; about the role of women (in the Baptist, Quaker, and other Separatist communities women had an increasingly important place but it was later among Quakers alone that women were fully accepted as having equal status in the worshipping group) and so on. Faction begat faction, as each group tried to establish its own particular truth.

As well as being overtly theological in nature, these conflicts were political and social in the widest sense. The whole question of how society could best be governed for the benefit of everyone was being raised and many of the answers given were radical. As George Fox travelled up and down the country, he met with others who also had spent time seeking for a more intimate relationship with God. This search was taking them away from the mainstream churches, and was eventually to lead to the founding of what is now known as the Religious Society of Friends.

These men and women who later became Friends, brought with them ideas they had found in the varying factions they had come from, and for a period the Quaker movement was a much less coherent body than it later became. In today's world of rapid change with fewer than one quarter of the members of the Society born of Quaker parents, we can see a parallel. The challenge to modern Quakerism is a similar one: how today to fuse ex-Baptists, ex-Anglicans, ex-atheists, ex-Buddhists, ex-practising Jews, ex-so many things, into a united society (though not a uniform one).

The Seventeenth Century

In the seventeenth century it was George Fox who put his stamp on this emerging group. It would be a mistake however to equate a movement with one man, charismatic though he may have been. Throughout the north Midlands and the North West, groups had already set themselves apart from the mainstream churches. Many of them met in silence without priest or pastor. Many of them already had rejected outward sacraments and were waiting for a new form of spirituality. John Punshon puts it this way in his chapter on the background of the earliest Friends:

The age of outward and formal religion was over. The age of scriptural bondage and sacramental symbolism was done. Worldly pride and ostentation were doomed. Power was draining away from the kingdoms of the world and into the restored kingdom of God, for Christ was here to teach his people himself.[12]

It was Fox with his administrative ability and Margaret Fell (1614-1702), who later became his wife, who were able to fuse these groups into a society which has survived, while most other religious groups originating at this time have died away. Yet the Quaker movement was not to be united easily. There were clashes of personality as well as of principles. James Nayler (1617-1660), whose enthusiasm and charisma sometimes led his followers to excess, clashed with Fox on a number of occasions. In the 1660's John Perrott, an Irish Friend from Waterford, protested against the increasing centralising of decision-making among Quakers and condemned the custom of removing hats when a Friend prayed aloud in meeting, and of shaking hands at the end of the meetings. This almost led to a schism, but in spite of these differences Quakers spread and grew and met greater persecution. Between 1650 and 1687, it has been estimated that 13,000 Friends were imprisoned, 198 were transported and 338 died in penal institutions or of wounds inflicted upon them while they were attending meeting.

Persecution did not cool the ardour of the men and women who left family and home to become 'publishers of Truth'. It is from this period that the Quaker custom of 'speaking truth to power' arises. In 1657 Mary Fisher (1623-1698), who had sailed to Massachusetts to witness for the truth, travelled to Constantinople to try to convince the Sultan. Others sought audience with the Pope and met with imprisonment or death at the hands of the Inquisition. Mary Dyer was hanged for her beliefs in 1660 on Boston Common by the very Puritans who had left England to find liberty of worship. But it was this revolutionary desire to publish the truth that God was immediately accessible to all human beings that eventually led to the founding in the seventeenth and eighteenth centuries of Quaker groups in centres throughout Europe, North America and the Caribbean.

The Eighteenth Century

Like most fervent movements, the Quaker movement began to lose something of its impetus as its founding members died. From being a movement to preach a new or regained truth it took on the characteristics of an inward-looking sect, handing down traditions and regulating the activities of its partisans. From being a revival of the true universal church, Friends now saw themselves as a remnant keeping precious their past insights. In the eighteenth and early nineteenth centuries they became a 'peculiar' people, suspicious of the outside world, wearing distinctive clothes, speaking a language full of distinctive jargon, addressing each other as 'thee' and 'thou', and although they still held public meetings now and again, very few newcomers were attracted to them.

But this introspection was not total, religious fervour had not died, and Friends were still concerned about conditions in the world around them. John Bellers (1654-1725), for instance, forms a link between the early persecutions and the subsequent period of retrenchment, yet he carried on the social witness of the first generation of Quakers with his schemes for the welfare of destitute children and in his writings he speaks of the 'labour of the poor being the mines of the rich'. His theories influenced later radicals such as Robert Owen and Karl Marx. Similarly

John Woolman was one of the first in the Society to condemn slavery, urge economic boycotts, and to care about conditions aboard ships. He also prompted Friends to see the connection between the way they lived, the possessions they owned and the violence and oppression which were part of the economic and political institutions of their day.

The interest some Friends showed in the social conditions of their day was matched by the fascination of other Friends for the natural world. If helping other people was a sign of the Christian life, the exploration of nature was a sign of human appreciation of a divinely inspired universe and the Quaker contribution was considerable. John Fothergill (1712-1780) played a notable role in the medical world; as did Peter Collinson (1694-1768) in botany. Towards the end of the period, John Dalton (1766-1844) and William Allen (1770-1843) made great contributions to chemistry. One of the most important discoveries of the eighteenth century, the smelting of iron by using coke rather than charcoal, was made by the Quaker, Abraham Darby (1678-1717), at Coalbrookdale in Shropshire. This and other inventions at Coalbrookdale had great bearing on the growth of the Industrial Revolution.

The Nineteenth Century

Gradually as the nineteenth century advanced Quakers began to look outwards from the small world of their own denomination as they were more and more open to religious and social insights from other traditions. The outside world had already witnessed the Methodist movement of which Quakers at first were very suspicious and yet this movement went on to influence most of the churches in one way or another. Some Quakers by the end of the eighteenth century, believed that their Society had become too complacent, too introspective, and like many in other churches felt the need for greater personal commitment. During this period, often described as the 'quietist' period of Quaker history, The Bible had been read in the home, but there was fear in the Society that too much reliance on it at worship would interfere with the still small voice in the heart. Under the impact of the evangelical movement and the teachings of the Quaker evangelical, Joseph John Gurney (1788-1847), these dissatisfied Quakers turned again to The Bible. They felt that without Biblical and doctrinal authority they were powerless to overcome the world of sin and separation and came eventually to place a greater emphasis than did their immediate forebears on personal salvation and the doctrine of atonement.

In this they realised that they were close to Christians of other persuasions and this led them to cross the barriers of distrust and to work with others to improve society around them. Again William Allen was typical of this movement. His work with the Anti-Slavery Society and with the London poor reveals how Quakers were taking their religious convictions into the public arena and were beginning to co-operate with other churches. Similarly Joseph Lancaster (1778-1838), one of the first advocates of popular education on a national scale, drew other non-conformists into a society that later became the British and Foreign Schools Society. One of the best known of all Quakers, Elizabeth Fry (1780-1845), belonged to an old Quaker family, the Gurneys. She seems at first to have worn her membership of the Society quite lightly, but she was converted to a more evangelical faith and the fervour of this faith led her to prison visiting and then to prison reform.

There was however a backlash in more conservative Quaker circles who were afraid that such worldly activity and evangelical theology would dilute Quakerism.

ELIZABETH FRY, portrait by George Richmond

Eventually these conflicts led Quakers in North America to split up into different factions. Some of these divisions still remain, although gatherings are held to broaden mutual understanding of the different Quaker traditions. Even today the conferences are not always easy affairs when theology is discussed, yet there is much greater co-operation than previously.

There has always been a possible tension among Quakers between, on the one hand, the idea that the leadings of the light within were sufficient for spiritual fulfilment and, on the other hand, a reliance on The Bible and the atonement for sins through the crucifixion of Jesus of Nazareth. This tension was brought to the surface by the evangelical emphasis on scriptural authority and the perceived need for salvation, a position held by many prominent Quakers towards the middle of the nineteenth century. Later in the nineteenth century, the tension grew into conflict as among some Friends the growing belief in the scientific method was leading to a reassessment of the nature of authority and historical accuracy. Texts were being studied and questioned, and Biblical infallibility, a belief close to the hearts of many an evangelical according to which The Bible was literally true, was no longer being taken for granted. This led to three distinct trends among Quakers: the traditionalists or conservatives, who quietly relied upon the Light of Christ within; the evangelicals for whom The Bible was growing in importance as a source of authority; and the new modernists or liberals whose theology was suspect to both of the others as it questioned both the distinctiveness of some of the old customs and the literalness of The Bible. Under the impact of the new biblical criticism and the work of Charles Darwin, the modernists were questioning their faith and were trying to see how the new knowledge fitted in with the old certainties. Whereas in the United States, these trends resulted in splits, in Britain there has been no comparable division.

The Twentieth Century Dawns

There was no doubt that for many (often contradictory) reasons, groups of Quakers were confused about the direction their Society was taking. This search for a new direction and revival came to a head in a national conference held in Manchester in 1895. Under the leading of John Wilhelm Rowntree (1868-1905), Quakers saw the need for a greater commitment to an understanding of the origins of their Society, to a new teaching ministry (which eventually led to the creation of Woodbrooke, the Quaker study centre in Birmingham), and to a new vision of the role of Quakers in the twentieth century.

This was on the whole a triumph for a more liberal, outward-going, emphasis but if it was a form of religious liberalism it was a liberalism enhanced by a mystical awareness of the presence of God. The notable exponent of this stream of Quakerism was the American, Rufus M. Jones (1863-1948). For him the personal experience of God is a mystical experience. In his *The Flowering of Mysticism*, he describes it thus: 'Mysticism is an immediate, intuitive, experimental knowledge of God, or one might say it is consciousness of a Beyond or of Transcendent Reality or of Divine Presence'[13]. The emphasis in this book is on the light within; less is placed on the historical crucifixion.

The last quarter of the twentieth century has brought about other transformations in the Society which I shall consider in Chapter 6. What is important about these different historical emphases in Quakerism is that to a varying extent they are all still alive in the Religious Society of Friends. There are still enthusiasts who wish to carry the message of George Fox to the market place; quietists who feel that too much outward activity gets in the way of the Spirit; evangelicals who witness to the effect in their lives of Jesus Christ, their saviour and redeemer; liberals whose gospel is a social one and whose emphasis is on a religious humanism; mystics who speak of the Spirit in all things; and others who would simply call themselves Christians, for whom no other title quite fits their understanding of religion. Indeed it is one of the joys, though not unmixed sometimes with anxiety, to have all these Quakers sitting down together in worship. For it is worship which brings Quakers together. And it is out of worship that arises the Quaker idea of service in the world.

Chapter Four

FROM CONVICTION TO PRACTICE:
FAITH INTO ACTION

A *body dies when it is separated from the Spirit, and in the same way faith is dead if it is separated from good deeds.*

The letter of James 2:26

Their religious convictions and worship do not lead Quakers away from the world but lead them back into it to look for the Spirit working there. There are two words which Quakers often use to describe the practical work which flows from their spiritual insights: concern and testimony.

Concern .

It is commonplace in daily speech to hear that people are concerned about particular matters: people are concerned about their children's future, nuclear energy, additives in food, the future of Africa, violence on television and so forth. They may not do much, if anything, about these matters, but they are worried and bothered. The word 'concern' has a more powerful meaning among Quakers. It refers to a religious compulsion to act in a certain way based on a 'leading of the Spirit'. Early Quakers left home and family under a concern to preach the truth as they saw it, just as Mary Fisher had a concern to speak to the Sultan or Elizabeth Fry to improve the condition of prisoners in Newgate prison. Similarly one could say that John Woolman had a concern about the possession and selling of slaves and felt compelled to act according to the dictates of the light within him. He brought this matter up time and time again as he travelled widely among fellow Quakers. It took quite some time before the whole Religious Society of Friends accepted his insight. Eventually however Quakers became the first group as a body to speak out against the whole institution of slavery.

These concerns, originally rising out of the experience of individual Quakers, were brought before the worshipping group to which he or she belonged. This is still the accepted procedure. The concern is thus put into focus, refined as it were, in a corporate search for the guidance of God and the group can then offer moral, spiritual, or financial support. Sometimes the group does not support the concern. It may ask the concerned Friend for further information or to reflect more deeply on the matter. Though the process may often seem slow and ponderous, it has enabled many Quakers to act wisely and faithfully in situations of uncertainty and even of danger.

I have often been quite impressed at how, by a sensitive listening to one another, Quakers have come to decisions which no one could have predicted at the outset. All this may take time, but that in itself is a good discipline. When it works well, everyone present can feel fully respected and listened to. Being part of the decision-making process, they can then support all the more the plans for carrying out the decision.

Testimony

'The very existence of the Religious Society of Friends may be seen as a testimony to the spontaneity of the relationship between human beings and God. It is a warning against institutionalism and the confinement of the human spirit.' It was not a Quaker who said that to me but a former abbot of an Anglican monastery.

The word 'testimony' is used by Quakers to describe a witness to the living truth within the human heart as it is acted out in everyday life. It is not a form of words, but a mode of life based on the realisation that there is that of God in everybody, that all human beings are equal, that all life is interconnected. It is affirmative but may lead to action that runs counter to certain practices currently accepted in society at large. Hence a pro-peace stance may become an anti-war protest, and a witness to the sanctity of human life may lead to protests against capital punishment. The testimonies reflect the corporate beliefs of the Society, however much individual Quakers may interpret them differently according to their own light. They are not optional extras, but fruits that grow from the very tree of faith. As early Friends would have put it, they are the outward signs of a restored relationship with God.

Although it is for the peace testimony that Friends are best known, this is only one aspect of living according to the dictates of truth. It was precisely an obedience to truth as they understood it that led Quakers to act in ways which others thought odd and even provocative. In 1659 Thomas Ellwood, a young Oxfordshire squire, was going about his business in Oxford when he met a group of his old friends who greeted him according to the courteous practices of the time. He stood there silently while his friends continued bowing, scraping, and taking off their hats. Finally they realised that a change had come over him:

> *they were amazed, and looked first one upon another, then upon me, and then one upon another again for a while, without a word speaking. At length, the surgeon ... clapping his hands, in a familiar way, upon my shoulder, and smiling on me, said, 'What, Tom! a Quaker?'* [14]

And Tom had not said a word! His whole manner of being would have told his friends that here was someone who did not treat others in an affected way, someone for whom the putting off of hats was an important matter (Quakers took off their hat for God alone in prayer), someone for whom words were important and not to be used lightly. Thomas Ellwood would have worn simple clothes, have used 'thee' and 'thou' to all people, and would have refused to address people by their titles. In a court of law he would not have taken an oath, for, as well as the Biblical commandment against swearing, and for letting your 'yea be yea and your nay be nay', there was the belief that all your words should be truthful and swearing an oath suggested two levels of truth. So your behaviour was your testimony of truth.

Of course as social customs change so the testimony to simplicity and integrity needs to be expressed in more relevant ways. It is hard to have a concern about 'hat honour' when most people do not wear hats and you cannot withhold tithes when a tenth of your income or produce does not go to the parish. But what about paying that proportion of taxes which goes towards military expenditure? That is an issue which is exercising a number of Friends today.

Nowadays Quakers no longer use 'thee' and 'thou' but are aware of the way they use language, especially recognising the need for gender-free terminology. It has even been suggested that the modern equivalent of the old plain speech is inclusive language, where one does not presume the masculine form includes the feminine. An example of this might be the use of 'people' or 'humanity' instead of the forms 'man' or 'mankind'.

The testimony against titles still holds; it includes the refusal to address each other with Mr, Miss or Mrs. Quakers call each other by their first names and family names, irrespective of age, material or social status. This is further witness to the equality of all people.

Integrity and Stewardship

To some the Quaker insistence on integrity, simplicity and truthfulness may seem off-putting and puritanical. To others it may seem hopelessly idealistic. Yet to others it is proof of a commitment to spiritual values. It has to be stressed again and again that these are the guidelines for everyday living rather than a description of it. In other words, Quakers are human beings with frailties like everyone else. Yet it is a fact that Quakers do have a sense of justice and honesty and are as a group quite idealistic. It is also part of their idea of testimony that their rejection of conventional approaches to a number of issues may well lead to suffering or simply to a reputation for impractical 'do-goodery'. They often feel able to act as they do because they feel that somehow and somewhere in the complexities of everyday life God is working with them and through them.

It may be one of life's ironies that integrity also pays. Looking at the rather anti-materialist stance of many modern Quakers, it is sometimes surprising to reflect that a number of large businesses were actually Quaker in origin and became successful because people could trust the company to be honest and faithful in its business dealings. Barclay's Bank, though no longer Quaker, grew in this way, as did Lloyd's. Similarly, the Friends' Provident Insurance was founded early in the nineteenth century and became one of the big insurance groups, but is now out of Quaker control.

When fortunes were amassed, the idea of responsible stewardship grew among the wealthy Quaker families, leading for example to the improvement of housing conditions for their workers. George Cadbury (1839-1922), a chocolate manufacturer, was also an adult school teacher, and he was keenly aware of the poor housing conditions of industrial workers. He founded Bournville Village which in turn influenced first the Garden City movement and then the planning of the post-Second World War new towns. Conditions in his factory were in the vanguard of enlightened industrial relations. The Cadbury and the Rowntree families, as well as the families of other Quaker industrialists, set up trusts which still give much practical support to groups, both Quaker and non-Quaker, whose interests lie in the creation of a more just and enlightened society.

On the other hand, the connections between the misuse of the earth's resources, economic exploitation and violence have been emphasised by Quakers as far back as John Woolman in his 'A Plea for the Poor':

> *O that we who declare against wars, and acknowledge our trust to be in God only, may walk in the light ... may we look upon our treasures and the furniture of our houses, and the garments in which we array ourselves, and try whether the seeds of war have any nourishment in these, our possessions.*[15]

This link is made today by Quakers looking at how the world economy is distorted by the vast expenditure on nuclear and other weapons, how much of the world suffers malnutrition, poor water supplies, hunger and drought, while fortunes are spent on non-useful commodities and armaments.

On a more humble level, the Quaker concern for the right ordering of the world's resources influences the way they use their own finances. Betting and gambling for example are very rare among Quakers and you will not find meetings organising raffles for funds. The principle here is one of using resources creatively and not gaining by other people's losses. This is particularly urgent today when many valuable social projects are dependent on money raised by the National Lottery. Quakers have spoken out against this form of national gambling and no Quaker project has accepted money from it.

Moderation

In view of the harm done by the use of alcohol, tobacco and other habit-forming drugs, consider whether you should limit your use of them or whether you should refrain from them altogether. Remember that any use of alcohol or drugs may impair judgement and place both the user and others in danger.[16]

So reads part of the *Advices*. You will note here that rules are not being set down. Some Quakers are teetotal, some drink in moderation. Some smoke, some refrain from all tobacco. The question is always: are you in control of your life, are you using your money wisely and creatively, are you setting an example to those over whom you have some influence? In this matter as in many others, it is easy to be carried away by social pressure and it is often hard to stick to principles.

Peace

A testimony is a lived experience, not a form of words. Often when talking about the peace testimony, Quakers refer to two extracts from George Fox from 1651 and 1661 which suggest that this experience was neatly formulated from the early days. The first statement by Fox was a refusal to take up a captaincy in Cromwell's army which was offered to him by Commonwealth Commissioners:

> *I told them I lived in the virtue of that life and power that took away the occasion of all wars ... I told them I was come into the covenant of peace which was before wars and strife were.* [17]

The second statement is part of a letter signed by a dozen prominent Quakers to Charles II disassociating Quakers from the uprising of the Fifth Monarchists and trying to prove to the King that Quakers should not be punished along with this other dissident body. The extract usually quoted begins:

> *We utterly deny all outward wars and strife and fighting with outward weapons, for any end or under any pretence whatsoever.* [18]

Yet to quote these two documents out of their context is rather misleading. There was a wide diversity among early Quakers about the nature of 'the peaceable kingdom'. Indeed in Scotland and Ireland, it was in the Commonwealth army garrisons that Quaker ideas spread most rapidly, and many Quakers left the army at first for refusing to take an oath rather than for refusing to fight. It was only gradually that a realisation took place that fighting was incompatible with Christian principles. This was not a once and for all revelation; neither is the peace testimony today a static creed among Quakers. It is often a hard fought inner battle and doubt remains over its consequences in the minds of many individuals.

There is no doubt that early Quakers' refusal to fight with outward weapons did not mean that conflict was to be avoided. Conflict was a part of life. If you wished to 'turn the world upside down' and bring it to a realisation that Christ was alive and God immediately accessible to all, then you would inevitably come into conflict with the authorities. But the weapons were those of truth and love, not the sword and fire.

In the eighteenth and nineteenth centuries, in the area now covered by Britain Yearly Meeting, the peace testimony was mainly a matter of making representation to government against particular wars, helping with relief work, and a refusal to rejoice at times of victory. Some Quakers were also active in organisations devoted to the furtherance of peace. It was not however something that affected the lives of most Quakers directly, just as warfare on the whole did not affect the majority of the population. Quakers aimed at living peaceably with their neighbours but being at peace for most of them was an extension of being part of the quiet in the land, minding one's own business, getting on with simple lives of integrity and where possible giving their leisure to philanthropy and adult education. In North America however the situation was different. Quaker settlers played a part in trying to mediate between the native Americans and the colonial settlers, often at great danger from both sides. They were also troubled by having to pay taxes to support a militia for the defence of settlements. In Pennsylvania, this conflict cost them the backing of the majority of the rest of the population and led them to abdicate power in the mid-eighteenth century.

The twentieth century has forced Quakers to look more closely at the whole nature and meaning of peace and at objections to war on grounds of conscience. The First World War saw large Quaker meetings in a number of prisons, when many of them refused to have anything to do with fighting whatsoever. Others took a relativist line and worked

A march to Chechnya, calling for an end to the war between Chechnya and Russia, partly organised by Quaker Peace & Service representatives in Moscow

in the Friends Ambulance Unit or the Friends War Victims Relief Committee. One or two Quakers did enlist believing that it was a just war. Some of these were disowned from the Society for taking this stance, but this was not universal. Indeed these three approaches are the ways in which Quakers do react to fighting; the absolutist who refuses to have anything to do with war: the relativist who, while condemning the fighting, tries to mitigate the consequences of it; the small minority who enlist because they feel that their principles lead them to take up arms against an evil greater than warfare itself. It must be stated however that the corporate witness of Quakers is that all warfare is against the will of God, who is a God of peace.

However peace is not simply the absence of war; it is a vision of human wholeness. It is the ideal of human beings finding fulfilment as individuals at personal, social and international levels. The many Quakers involved in counselling and marriage guidance today are a witness to the fact that reconciliation between people is part of the peace testimony. This principle also underlies the work of the Quaker offices in New York and Geneva which represent Quaker views to the United Nations, and the office in Brussels which presents Quaker views to the Council of Europe and the European Union. Bringing together estranged partners, bringing together diplomats from apparently opposing nations, bringing together opposing social groups and hostile minorities are aspects of the comprehensive Quaker concept of peace.

During the last few years, some Quakers have been led to consider the need for non-violent direct action, to examine how much their finances actually pay for armaments, to consider how feminist thinking can liberate men from the need to work out their insecurities on the battlefield and to view the peace testimony as going beyond the human race to include the whole of creation. The end of the twentieth century is a fruitful and exciting period in the history of the Quaker witness to peace, made more immediate by the dire threat hanging over the world in the shape of the nuclear bomb and environmental disaster. The challenge is greater than ever, but Quakers believe that God is involved in this challenge.

Reconciliation

The demands of justice often seem opposed to the need for reconciliation. What passes for peace may really be the silence of the oppressed. It would be too easy to dismiss

Quaker concerns as simplistic or not grounded in the real world. The Quaker attitude is not one of keeping hands clean and saying 'we'll have nothing to do with this evil'. It is often a matter of being involved in negotiations before violence breaks out.

NOBEL PEACE PRIZE, gold medallion: obverse

Quaker internationalism has led to support for international bodies such as the old League of Nations and the United Nations of today. It is here that Quakers feel many international disputes could be resolved without recourse to violence. Quakers sometimes act as mediators receiving the confidence of opposing sides as in the Nigerian-Biafran war and the negotiations for the foundation of modern Zimbabwe. They have also been involved in the relief work after warfare has ended, as in France, Germany and eastern Europe after both World Wars. In more recent times they have worked among members of mutually suspicious communities as in Sri Lanka and Croatia. In working to remove the seeds of war and trying to help alleviate the mess brought about by warfare, Quakers have seen the connection between warfare and injustice, and realise that peace is often a slow process and needs constant vigilance. It was for their work in this sphere that the British Friends Service Council, together with the American Friends Service Committee, were awarded the Nobel Peace Prize in 1947.

Economic and Social Justice
This religious/political idea has forced Quakers to look at the whole of society and to consider the relationship between ideal and practice. At the present time (1996), there is a revival in concern about our social testimony and its radical implications for action. A number of Quakers are involved in politics in one way or another as a practical consequence of their religious convictions, though it must be pointed out that quite a few other Quakers have certain suspicions about too great an involvement in party politics.

This concern for social justice may be summed up in one of the *Advices*:

Seek to understand the causes of injustice, social unrest and fear. Are you working to bring about a just and compassionate society which allows everyone to develop their capacities and fosters the desire to serve? [19]

At a time when unemployment is becoming the way of life for many and alienation grows apace, Quakers are considering the whole concept of 'work' and a few Meetings are beginning to sponsor projects for unemployed people.

The injustice felt by large sections of the community is compounded by racism and prejudice against ethnic and other minorities. One Quaker poster announces that 'Variety is the Spice of Life' and yet, for many people, variety is threatening and increases insecurity. Hence the need today to proclaim with great vigour the message that there is that of God in everyone and that each individual has worth irrespective of colour, race, religion, sex, and occupation (paid or unpaid).

Penal Reform

In the early days of persecution, thousands of Quakers were jailed and hundreds died in prison. Earlier this century many went to prison as conscientious objectors. Today some Quakers face prison again as they protest against arms bases and taxation for weapons of mass destruction. This has given them some knowledge of prison life and a desire to reform conditions. Elizabeth Fry for example spent much of her time campaigning for literacy, privacy and better clothing for the women of Newgate Prison and the prisoners in general. Many a time she waited with women soon to be hanged, trying to console them in their last hours.

Throughout their history Quakers have campaigned against capital punishment as a denial of God's power to work in every man and woman. The emphasis today is on work with offenders in the probation and other services and on trying to help them find a place in the community after their release as in the centre for ex-offenders run by Quakers in Liverpool. Writing to prisoners on death row, being a human contact at a time of great distress is another way Quakers try to bring light into the darkness.

Education and Social Responsibility

Education is a matter of bringing out the potential of the individual and fostering an openness to experience. Quakers have long seen how important this process is and they are engaged in all aspects of the educational system. The majority of Quaker teachers work in state schools, but some teach in the eight schools run by the Society in England, most of which are co-educational. (Most of the pupils and teachers however are not Quakers.) In these schools the academic side of life is respected but it is the development of the whole personality which is the main goal. This includes the encouragement of artistic and practical skills. Many Quakers have also been involved in running progressive schools because they felt that certain aspects of education were not provided for elsewhere.

Woodbrooke in Birmingham is an international Quaker centre for adult education. It is residential and offers short and long term courses on a wide range of issues covering Quaker, Christian, interfaith, social and international studies. A number of Quaker meeting houses also serve as adult education centres and are used by a variety of organisations for educational purposes.

Children at a school in Hackney, London, where Quakers
have organised peace education lessons

To respond to the concerns of individual Quakers up
and down the country, committees and groups have been
set up to study for example the social implications of
housing and unemployment, economic, racial and criminal
justice, and truth and integrity in public affairs. Thus the
practical approach is based on study, analysis and
experience. The kingdom of heaven grows from hard work
as well as inspiration.

Work Abroad

Some years ago I travelled round Southern Africa visiting
various Quaker projects. I noticed then one or two
significant characteristics of this sort of work. The main
aim was to respect the dignity and independence of the
people with whom Quakers were working. In these projects,
the Quakers and their representatives were not acting as
traditional missionaries, but rather as partners with an
emphasis on sharing and helping people to help
themselves. At the time there was an agricultural centre

69

near Bulawayo in southern Zimbabwe. The Quakers involved were trying out simple forms of technology which did not rely on foreign spare parts and which could therefore be replaced easily. In addition to this, new plants were being introduced into the area to supply better sources of nutrition. A school had been opened and the workers were spending a lot of their time taking the new ideas into the rural areas to help the surrounding villages.

I found the same caring in a different project further south in Botswana, where refugees from countries with differing regimes had come together to escape oppression at home and to carry on with their education. As this refugee centre was situated in a village outside the capital, it was necessary to reconcile the differing perceptions of the villagers with those of the refugees, whom they distrusted. Education, help for the oppressed, and reconciliation, three traditional areas of Quaker concern, were fused in a comparatively small but vital enterprise. The centre is no longer run by Quakers but the Quaker ethos persists.

The projects have changed over the years and the emphasis has moved from relief work to supporting small-scale enterprises, where people can help themselves and regain their dignity. Other schemes run, sponsored, or funded by Quakers are educational, agricultural or medical in emphasis. British Quakers and their representatives have been working in several countries in Africa, Asia, Latin America and the Middle East as well as closer to home in mainland Europe. Often the Quaker presence is small and limited, but it is a witness to the need for peace and justice, and the respect due to all human beings.

Building Bridges of Co-Operation

Brummana Friends pack kitchen kits for refugees in South Lebanon

Quaker work camps, now known as Quaker International Social Projects, began after the First World War. The main aim was reconciliation through reconstruction. Nowadays the projects tend to last for one to three weeks, and half the group comes from Britain and the other half from the mainland of Europe and sometimes beyond; a few volunteers are Quakers, but most are not. The Quaker witness to bridge-building and care for the community is maintained in a very practical way and the work that is undertaken is work that otherwise might not be done. Over the years many international friendships have been built up as people have got to know each other while working positively for local communities.

Chapter Five

QUAKER ORGANISATION:
MEETINGS AND MEETINGS

*N*ew religious movements often claim to be reviving old truths hidden under the dead weight of tradition. They create new structures to help them better to live out these truths in their new communities. But after a few years the founders die out and the next generation receives the wisdom secondhand and takes for granted the structures which the old pioneers struggled to evolve. As the movement loses some of its dynamism, the members rely more and more on organisation to carry them through. Soon these very structures are seen to be getting in the way of true life and a new movement comes into being to reform them.

This has happened among Quakers, yet the Religious Society of Friends has survived because it has had wise administrators and, from its early days, a structure based on the needs of its members. It is the paradox and the challenge of practical mysticism.

This chapter is an attempt to introduce Britain Yearly Meeting from the point of view of its organisation. It is a simplification and it takes years before Quakers themselves fully understand its nature. My work in Friends House, London, has brought me in contact with many committees whose names range from the obviously named Social Justice Committee to the more obscure Six Weeks Meeting Committee (which deals with the premises of London meeting houses). The trouble is often that as soon as one has understood one set of names, the committees seem to change their names or cease to function or amalgamate!

Meetings in Britain

BRITAIN YEARLY MEETING covers England, Scotland and Wales, with the Isle of Man and the Channel Islands. Within this there are almost 490 local meetings, most of which are called Preparative Meetings. These form larger units known as Monthly Meetings, of which there are seventy-two. Monthly Meetings are part of yet larger units called GENERAL MEETINGS. There are seventeen of these.

PREPARATIVE MEETINGS (so called because they prepare business for the Monthly Meeting) may vary in size. Some may have fewer than 10, others as many as 200 members - and in addition they usually have a number of attenders attached to them. As there are no clergy, all members have a responsibility for the life of the Meeting, but each Preparative Meeting will have a Clerk, and most will also have Elders, Overseers and a Treasurer and a few committees to help them carry out their responsibilities.

The MONTHLY MEETING is the primary business meeting of the Society. Here membership is decided upon, so that when an attender becomes a Quaker she or he is accepted into membership by the local Monthly Meeting. The Monthly Meeting is also the body responsible for, amongst other things, the right and regular holding of meetings for worship in its constituent Preparative Meetings, the appointment of Elders and Overseers, the maintenance of a register of members, and applications for membership. It also has responsibility for the supervision of weddings and funerals, and the appointment of prison ministers, hospital visitors and representatives to various other organisations.

The Clerk and the Business Meeting

Every Preparative Meeting has its Clerk. The Clerk of the Meeting usually reads the notices at the end of meeting for worship. He or she presides over the business meetings and serves as a sort of combined chairperson and secretary. The business the Preparative Meeting might discuss could be whether to make a donation to a particular charity, what activities to pursue in the local community, matters concerning the premises, whether to organise an exhibition in the town to make Quakers better known or how to write to the local Member of Parliament about an issue which is worrying the Meeting.

Quaker business meetings at Preparative, Monthly or Yearly Meeting level are held in the context of worship. They may take place after meeting for worship on a Sunday or at any other convenient time during the week. Attenders may join in as well with the permission of the Clerk of the Meeting. The aim of the business meeting is to discover the will of God. It is not a matter of bowing to the will of majorities or minorities, and Quakers do not vote: rather it is an exercise of listening to God through what each person says.

The Clerk discerns 'the sense of the meeting' and writes a minute which must receive there and then the assent, spoken or tacit, of the meeting. Do not be surprised to hear the Quaker phrase 'hope so' or 'I hope so' intoned by one or two experienced Friends present. They are saying that they hope the minute will be acceptable to the meeting. If no sense of the meeting is discerned, no decision will be taken, and no minute will be made except to record that the meeting is not ready to proceed.

Elders and Overseers

Elders and Overseers, of whom there will usually be several in each Meeting, are appointed by Monthly Meeting. These appointments are made usually for a three-year period. The most visible role the elders have in meeting is for two of them to shake hands to signal the end of meeting for worship. They have a particular responsibility for the spiritual life of the Meeting. This may mean organising Bible study, discussion groups and meetings for newcomers and other outreach work - in short, the education of the whole meeting including children.

Overseers have more of a pastoral responsibility for the members and attenders. They give advice and information about application for membership and help with any personal difficulties that the worshippers may be encountering. They also keep in touch with people who cannot attend regularly or who are rarely, if ever, seen at meeting.

Both these roles call for great sensitivity as they are the practical implementation of the Quaker conviction that there is divine potential in everyone which needs nurturing and fostering. In a number of Meetings, people are appointed to a dual role of elder/overseer; in one or two places the roles have been abolished because it is considered that everybody is responsible; but however the matter is dealt with, a real community is one based on worship and shows itself in caring.

General Meetings

The main purpose of the GENERAL MEETING which meets up to three times a year is 'for conference and inspiration, and for a broad oversight of the life and witness of the Society within its area'. Here there is much less emphasis on business and more on discussion of topics of general interest to the Society.

The General Meeting area may cover a large part of the country. For example Western General Meeting covers an area from Aberystwyth to Shrewsbury in the north and Milford Haven to Cirencester in the south. Quakers are used to travelling for conferences and meeting each other, but poor rural transport and difficulties for the elderly often prevent some people from attending. Recently the Meeting of Friends in Wales has been founded to take into account the need for a Welsh entity. However the problem of accessibility remains here as elsewhere.

It must be emphasised that Quakers realise people have many different calls on their time and there is no compulsion or pressure to attend all these meetings. At some periods in their lives people are freer than at others. There is however a commitment on the part of members to help when and as they can.

Yearly Meeting

In the nineteenth century, one (undeclared) function of YEARLY MEETING was to bring together young Quakers with a view to matrimony. I am sure that in one or two cases it may still have this function but Yearly Meeting as an annual gathering of up to eighteen hundred Quakers is still quite an event. Any business that needs a corporate decision is discussed at the large sessions and at its best the involvement of so many people in decision-making is a wonder to behold.

In addition to decision-making sessions, Yearly Meeting has in recent years considered more general questions such as international relations, worship and our social testimony, our caring for the planet and its resources, the spiritual depth of Society, the right holding of business meetings, simplicity and homelessness, and the role of young people in the Society. However fellowship is important and Quakers do actually enjoy themselves at these occasions, meeting old friends, and making new ones. In recent years they have felt freer to celebrate the moving of the Spirit amongst them in song, dance, and drama as well as in the more traditional ways.

Meeting for Sufferings and Friends House

Of course there are difficulties when so many people are involved. Policy items which need a quicker response are resolved by the Yearly Meeting's standing executive committee known as MEETING FOR SUFFERINGS. The name derives from the recording by this committee, in the seventeenth-century, of the sufferings and persecutions of Quakers for their religious convictions. 'Sufferings', as it is generally known in the Society of Friends, meets eight to ten times a year in Friends House in London and has representatives from each Monthly Meeting.

Friends House contains also the central offices of Britain Yearly Meeting and its library. The various departments here are responsible to Meeting for Sufferings. The Recording Clerk's office oversees the various departments and services both Meeting for Sufferings and Yearly Meeting. The three departments carrying out work for the whole of the Yearly Meeting are QUAKER PEACE & SERVICE, which is responsible for community development, the agricultural, medical and aid work abroad as well as for peace activities at home and abroad; QUAKER SOCIAL RESPONSIBILITY & EDUCATION, which is responsible for social affairs, penal reform, community relations, homes for the aged, education and so forth; and QUAKER HOME SERVICE which co-ordinates religious education within the Society from 'cradle to the grave', outreach, work with enquirers, children and young people's activities. It also publishes literature to nurture the spiritual life of the Society. Quaker Home Service also has responsibility for the QUAKER BOOKSHOP, a shop open to the general public which stocks a wide range of Quaker and other religious material. There are also departments for communication with the Society's membership, service of the premises, fundraising, personnel, and finance.

Information about any of these can be obtained from Friends House, Euston Road, London NW1 2BJ; telephone: 0171-387-3601.

Next door to Friends House is Drayton House, in which is to be found the editorial office of *The Friend*, an independent weekly publication which mirrors the range of thinking among Quakers in Britain today. Nearby in Byng Place can be found THE FRIENDS WORLD COMMITTEE FOR CONSULTATION, which links the various Yearly Meetings throughout the world. Quakers have always been great travellers and they keep in touch, especially with smaller groups scattered throughout the world.

Chapter Six

QUAKERS TODAY:

RESPECT FOR DIVERSITY

I remember being present at a residential Yearly Meeting attended by over two thousand Quakers - quite a daunting experience. This was the largest ever gathering of Britain Yearly Meeting. Some of the more introverted Quakers were a little apprehensive but the friendly mixture of bustle and silence satisfied most of them. Important decisions were taken, such as on the role of Quakers within the Christian tradition - after lively contributions concerning the wording of the text - a Quaker response to the Baptism, Eucharist, and Ministry report of the World Council of Churches was approved. The Quaker business method still worked even with so vast a throng.

There was also at this Yearly Meeting a presentation on the role of women and their oppression in society in general, sessions on human rights at home and abroad, on human relationships and sexuality; there was a peace vigil and a celebration which took up all the themes of the week's activities. However intense the darkness that overshadows the world may sometimes seem, Quakers believe that the light is still there and there is still the time and the need for celebration.

Informal Groups

On the fringe of the main sessions of Yearly Meeting are held smaller gatherings devoted to particular issues and concerns of groups of Quakers. One such gathering I attended on this occasion was an introduction to various Quaker informal groups: THE FRIENDS INTER-FAITH GROUP, which, now under the wing of the QUAKER COMMITTEE FOR CHRISTIAN & INTERFAITH RELATIONS, organises meetings between representatives of different religions; the NEW FOUNDATION FELLOWSHIP which considers the life and writings of George Fox, and sees them as a model for a renewal of an energetic Christian Quakerism for today; the OPEN LETTER MOVEMENT and the SEEKERS' ASSOCIATION which aim through literature to challenge modern Quakerism to explore creatively contemporary thinking in philosophy, psychology, and theology. Also present were the QUAKER UNIVERSALISTS who emphasise that all religious traditions are valid ways to God; representatives of the YOUNG FRIENDS CENTRAL COMMITTEE (now Young Friends General Meeting), a loosely constituted organisation most of whose members are in the eighteen to thirty age-range (liberally interpreted) and which acts as a vital link between many of the younger members and attenders of the Society; and the QUAKER SOCIALIST SOCIETY, which while non party-political, sees the work for democratic socialism as a vital aspect of its members' Quaker faith. And this was simply an introduction to the twenty or more groups in the Society.

Friends come together as women, healers, Esperantists, historians, teachers, homosexuals, teetotallers, vegetarians, campers, artists, world citizens, land value reformers, medics, and criminal justice reformers, amongst others. In fact I sometimes feel that if there is an interest, some Friend has set up a group for it. Recent years have seen the birth of new groups concerned with sexual abuse, ecology, and the promotion of quiet retreats. But to be a Quaker does not mean that you have to join yet another group or committee. The fact is that many Quakers do like being with similar-minded people, but many others enjoy attending meeting for worship on a Sunday and cannot or do not wish to spend time on these other activities.

The Society today is quite different from what it was a hundred, fifty or even twenty-five years ago. Social pressures have been felt by Quakers as by everyone else. Today as in probably no other period of their history since the seventeenth century, most Quakers were not born into the Society but joined as adults. Hence there has been a subtle change in the ethos of the Society. There is a greater openness to the world around and its culture and probably a loss of knowledge about Quaker traditions and ways of doing things. On the other hand there is a growing awareness of the need for renewal. Society at large is experiencing a hunger for spiritual values in reaction to the growth of materialistic attitudes. It is out of this hunger that many enquirers turn to the Religious Society of Friends and it must be admitted that Quakers are not always able to respond to this hunger. They tend to be tentative in the expression of their beliefs, and are concerned not to force them onto others, but this often seems like a lack of enthusiasm.

There is a growing awareness today among Quakers of the need to deepen and broaden the witness for peace: to see how the exploitation of our planet, the abuses of genetic engineering, the oppression of minority groups and of women (who in fact constitute a majority), the destruction of many species of animals, the reliance on fuels which may have dangerous consequences for whole communities and societies (expressed in the preoccupations of QUAKER GREEN CONCERN), are all part of human alienation and result from a lack of the vision that all creation is of God and should be cherished as such. I see these issues as the ones that are to the fore in contemporary Quakerism.

With this goes the respect for the diversity of all people and of life-styles. The Society today reflects social trends prevalent in society at large. Unemployment and divorce have both made inroads into modern Quaker families and one-parent families and alternative ways of living are much more widespread than in former years.

The stigma attached to divorce, to separation, to being gay or lesbian, is much less common and indeed in recent years the QUAKER LESBIAN AND GAY FELLOWSHIP has done much to support homosexual Quakers and attenders and to help them to accept themselves as full members of the Society of Friends. Not all Quakers have been able to overcome prejudice, but then few human beings can admit to being totally open to groups they have difficulty in understanding or of whom they have had perhaps little or no experience. Having written this, it has been my experience among Quakers that the vast majority have an openness to that of God in everyone to a degree that I have not found elsewhere.

photo Andrew Backhouse

Participants at JUNIOR YEARLY MEETING refurbishing tools for Tanzania

Young Friends

One of the trends in recent years that has worried many Quakers, and indeed other churches, is the disappearance of younger people from meeting. As adolescence draws on, religion seems to become boring to many people, however open that religion may be. Indeed it may be said that one of the problems of younger Quakers is that their parents are often so liberal that they do not provide the resistance that young people like to rebel against.

One of the more recent developments in the Society is the formation of LINK GROUPS. These link up young people over the age of twelve from a wide area for social gatherings as well as more serious day events and residential weekends. These groups try out experimental forms of worship and discuss topics which are raised by the young people themselves.

Quaker Home Service, through its Youthwork Secretaries, offers support, resources and training events, both at local and national level, to encourage and develop work with young people. It also organises the annual, national, four-day conference for sixteen to eighteen year old young Friends - JUNIOR YEARLY MEETING - where the leadership roles are taken by young people themselves. This renewal of life and liveliness among these young people is reflected also in THE LEAVENERS, the Quaker Youth Theatre, whose dramatic productions have generated a great spirit of fellowship and fun in its participants and have brought the themes of spiritual depth and the need for celebration before the Society as a whole.

'Young Friends', mentioned earlier, also provide an important support group for people in the eighteen to thirty age range. They organise national gatherings, appeals, and local discussion groups and are often the means of

QUAKER YOUTH THEATRE performs the music-drama,
The Banner and Blackshirts

enabling younger Friends, attenders and sympathisers to
play a full role in the life of the Society. Indeed it is through
the inspiration that they have found at gatherings that a
number of younger people have made their way into the
Society.

Chapter Seven

BEING PART OF A COMMUNITY:
MEMBERSHIP AND COMMITMENT

*I*f you go to meeting you will be hard pressed to tell who is the Friend and who the attender. (It really troubles me when I hear people saying 'I'm only an attender', no-one is 'only' anything.) If there is no spiritual distinction between member and attender, the question is asked, 'Why have membership at all?'

Membership

Among the early Friends membership was seen as commitment to the promptings of the voice of Christ or the inward light as expressed in daily life. The universalist tendency among many Quakers, which stresses that all religions are illuminated with God's light, has led some to assert that there is no point in identifying too closely with one particular group. Quakers today would not dream of saying that truth was alive only among Friends. To become a Quaker is not a matter of saying here alone is all truth. It is to say: 'This is where I as an individual feel at home. Here I can worship in a way that leads me to fulfilment. Here I can find others who share my seeking and my finding. This is my community.' It is not a matter of being 'good enough' or 'intelligent enough', or even having this or that exact view about Jesus of Nazareth. It is a matter of believing that the relationship between the self, the community, and God are best expressed for you among these people. This is not to say that this relationship cannot be expressed elsewhere; a number of Quakers do worship in other places as well as in the meeting house. Membership does not lead Quakers to live only in the Quaker compound, as it were, but is a matter of making a public witness to the truth as they see it.

George Gorman, in his *Introducing Quakers*, states this very well:

> *Membership of the Society is not a mere formality, but is the outward sign of a truly personal involvement with a group of people who share common convictions about the meaning and purpose of life. These arise from the still centre of their being and in their sense of identity with others when they are open to them in loving relationships ... Their involvement in this turns them out again to the wider community.*[20]

Functional Membership

There are functional as well as spiritual reasons for formal membership. Quakers have to decide matters for themselves and carry out these decisions on a whole range of issues. Any such group needs people who publicly commit themselves to the work and to be responsible for it. Long before formal membership got off the ground, Quaker committees were set up to consider any matters that confronted the Quaker community. By becoming Quakers today new members are saying that, if they have the time and energy, they will agree to take on responsibility for a certain aspect of Quaker life. Circumstances change and they may be able to do today what was impossible yesterday, and vice versa. Formal membership indicates at least a willingness to consider such duties. Certain Meetings I know are unwilling to ask attenders to take on responsibilities, because they feel this might be an imposition on them. Other Meetings on the other hand have to do so as there may be far more attenders than members and it seems that the attenders appreciate taking on these responsibilities.

Of course one of the responsibilities is the financial one. Just as the decisions taken within the Society are the decisions of its members, so the work carried out by the Society has to be paid for by them. Each meeting has a treasurer who will advise the member on his or her contribution. Unemployment and domestic difficulties hit Quakers like everyone else and it is recognised that some people can offer more than others. Quakers give what they can and giving can always be altered according to circumstances. Many members pay by covenant which enables the Society to benefit from tax relief.

These responsibilities often extend beyond the local Meeting. Because Quakers are so small a body it is often quite easy to know many of the extended Quaker family beyond regional boundaries. My own job working with enquirers makes it important for me to know that there is a group of committed Quakers in various areas to whom to refer new enquirers. Thus the members in that area act as the visible representatives of Quakers and are making a witness to Quaker insights and ways of living. So membership becomes not only a commitment to the group but a witness to society at large. This does not mean that you become a walking encyclopedia of the highways and byways of Quaker theology and folklore, nor an example of outstanding virtue and righteousness. It does mean that you are saying that Quakers are still alive and (pacifically) kicking and have a viewpoint that is very worth stating.

From Enquirer to Friend

We all remain enquirers for most of our lives. The journey stops at death and then probably only changes direction. But in Quaker jargon an 'enquirer' is someone who is new to the Society and possibly has only once or twice ever visited a meeting, if at all. A 'visitor' is someone who is a newcomer to Meeting or a member of another Meeting.

Most people who come to Meeting do so because they have met a Quaker or have read some introductory literature. The journey to the Religious Society of Friends can be a long, complicated and circuitous one. It is often with trepidation that the newcomer crosses the threshold of the meeting house. This may be the first and only visit or else the first of many. It is when it feels right and the attender has the feeling of being at home that he or she may feel the desire or need actually to join.

Enquirers at Charney Manor during a weekend conference

Getting to Know More

Enthusiasm is fine, but becoming a member is rather like a marriage. There may be the shyness or the flirtation, the infatuation, the going steady, but the marriage begins over the coffee-cups and the newspaper when the ceremony is over. It is only right that both partners get to know each other well to avoid disillusionment. It is advisable to attend over a period of time to become familiar with the Meeting. In this way enquirers will get to know the community and have the time to ask all those questions that they felt they could not ask when they first went to meeting. New questions crop up all the time. Not everyone in the Meeting knows the answer. It is a bit like tourists in London asking the way to St. Paul's. Sometimes the answer is 'I'm new myself' or 'the best person to ask is so-and-so'.

Secondly, it is useful to bear in mind that you do not join the local Meeting but the Monthly Meeting; in a sense you join the whole Society. So get to know as much of it as you can, by going to several different meetings for worship. Each Meeting has a different feel to it. If you live in a large city it is of course easier to visit several different Meetings than in other places, but on holiday you may well find there is a Meeting in the town and a visit will probably be worthwhile.

If further help is needed before joining, you could contact an Elder or Overseer of the Meeting or else borrow some books from the meeting house library. Quaker Home Service will be delighted to provide any information needed and, if you are in London, a visit to the Quaker Bookshop or the library will provide you with many valuable resources.

Quaker Home Service publishes *Quaker Monthly* with enquirers particularly in mind. It also organises weekend enquirers' gatherings at Charney Manor, a beautiful medieval manor house, southwest of Oxford. Weekend and one day gatherings are also held in other centres around the country both by QHS and local meetings.

CHARNEY MANOR, Oxfordshire. A Quaker house for conferences, retreats and study-weekends

Application for Membership

So finally you may decide to join. It is best at first to discuss this decision with one or two members of your home meeting. Then you send a letter to the Clerk of the Monthly Meeting containing a few details about the contacts you have with the local Meeting. The letter will go to a session of Monthly Meeting which will appoint two Quakers to visit you. One of these visitors will be known to you from the local Meeting, the other will usually come from another Meeting. The basic idea behind this visit is to give you the opportunity of asking questions in a relaxed and informal atmosphere, to find out whether you will feel at home among Quakers, and whether you are committed to basic Quaker attitudes. Several enquirers have told me that they felt they were going to be tested, but in fact they enjoyed the experience of an informal conversation in their own home. Of course we are all afraid of rejection. Most people are accepted, but if it is felt that the applicant really has too little experience of Meeting, or that his or her attitudes are really at odds with Friends, then the applicant is usually asked to wait and apply again later after having had more experience of the ways of Quakers. This is not a matter of being rejected, more a matter of honesty and an understanding of the nature of commitment.

The visitors then go back to Monthly Meeting and tell the Friends there about their discussion. Of course confidentiality is respected. There is no welcoming ceremony as such for the new member but the Meeting often expresses its pleasure in a very real and delighted way.

Because Quakers are such a diverse bunch of people, there is no attempt to make anyone conform. Indeed Quakers seem temperamentally nonconformist. On the other hand of course, there is always the danger of institutionalism in any group which has members and a structure. This is a very human weakness, but for all the talk of the smallness of the Society, its committees and its peculiar meetings, it remains a vital force which still says what always needs to be said: there is a power of love that overcomes everything and that lives in the hearts of all human beings. This love was in the life of Jesus of Nazareth and is seen in the lives of many people of all religions or of none.

This power is alive in each one of us; it can demand from us a deep commitment, and can challenge the way we live, treat others and care for our planet. It is a source of joy and freedom as it reveals to us our divine potential. Above all, it empowers us as we respond to it in worship. The light that illuminates us is the light that illuminates all of creation. IT IS THE LIGHT THAT IS ETERNALLY SHINING.

REFERENCES

1   Elizabeth Kübler-Ross, *Death, the Final Stage of Growth.* Englewood Cliffs, NJ, USA, Prentice Hall, 1975, p.164

2   William Penn, *A Collection of the Works of William Penn.* London, 1726, II, p.781

3   George Fox, *The Journal of George Fox* ed. J. L. Nickalls. London, Cambridge University Press, 1952; London Yearly Meeting, rptd. 1975, p.19

4   Elie Wiesel, *Night.* trs. S. Rodway. Harmondsworth, Middx., Penguin Books, 1981

5   Isaac Penington, *The Light Within and Selected Writings of Isaac Penington.* Philadelphia, Pa., USA,Tract Association of Friends, n.d., p.2

6   Lewis Benson, *George Fox's Message is Relevant Today.* New Foundation Publication 2, 1977

7   Robert Barclay, *Apology.* Proposition 10, section 2. London, 1678, pp. 181-2

8   *Ibid.*

9   *Advices & Queries.* Britain Yearly Meeting, 1994

10 Caroline Stephen, *Quaker Strongholds.*, London, Friends Home Service Committee, 1908 rptd. 1966, p.8

11   Thomas Kelly, *The Gathered Meeting.* London: Friends Home Service Committee, 1944, p.12, also *Reality of the Spiritual World and The Gathered Meeting.* London, Friends Home Service Committee, 1965, p. 49, new edition 1996.

12   John Punshon, *Portrait in Grey.* London, Quaker Home Service, 1984, p. 37

13   Rufus M. Jones, *The Flowering of Mysticism.* New York, USA, Macmillan, 1939, p.251

14   Thomas Ellwood, *History of the Life of Thomas Ellwood...Written by His Own Hand* (1714) ed. C.G. Crump. London, Methuen, 1900, pp. 23-4

15   John Woolman, 'A Plea for the Poor,' quoted in *The Wisdom of John Woolman* by Reginald Reynolds. 1948, Quaker Home Service, rptd. 1988, p. 142

16   *Advices & Queries, op. cit.* section 40

17   George Fox, *Journal, op. cit.,* p.65

18   *Ibid.,* pp. 399-400

19   *Advices and Queries, op. cit.* p. 20

20   George H. Gorman, *Introducing Quakers.* London, Quaker Home Service, 1969 last revised rpt. 1981, p. 72

FURTHER READING

Advices and Queries, Britain Yearly Meeting 1994.

Quaker Faith & Practice, Britain Yearly Meeting 1994.

Quaker by Convincement, Geoffrey Hubbard, QHS revised reprint 1992.

Yours in Friendship, Richard Allen, QHS 1995.

HISTORY

The Journal of George Fox editor John Nickalls, Philadelphia Yearly Meeting 1995.

George Fox and the Quakers, Cecil W Sharman, QHS 1991.

Portrait in Grey: a short history of the Quakers, John Punshon, QHS 1984, rev. rpt. 1991.

Quakers in Britain - a century of change 1895-1995, Alastair Heron, Curlew Graphics 1995.

WORSHIP & PRAYER

The Amazing Fact of Quaker Worship, George Gorman, QHS 1973, rpt. 1993.

Encounter with Silence: reflections from the Quaker Tradition, John Punshon, QHS 1987.

An Exercise of the Spirit: Quakers and prayer, compiled by Leila Ward. Edited by Ruth W Bell and Anne Hosking, QHS 1984.

God is Silence, Pierre Lacout, QHS 1970, rptd. 1993.

Silence and Speech, Richard Allen, QHS 1993.

THE BIBLE
Twenty Questions About Jesus, John Lampen, QHS 1985, rptd. 1994.

Is the Bible Important Today? If so, why?, Kenneth Lawton, Joseph Pickvance and John Waters, QHS 1995.

CHILDREN & YOUNG PEOPLE
A Portrait of Friends - an introduction to the Quakers for young people, Harvey Gillman, QHS 1993.

The Peace Kit: everyday peacemaking for young people, John Lampen, QHS 1992.

QUAKER WORK & WITNESS
Quaker Encounters: A study of two centuries of Quaker activity in the relief of suffering caused by war or natural calamity, Ormerod Greenwood, Sessions 1975-1978. In three volumes: *Friends and Relief, Vines on the Mountain* and *Whispers of Truth.*

Peace in the Power and the Light, David Lonsdale, QHS 1988.

Peace is a Process, Sydney D Bailey, QHS and Woodbrooke College 1993.

The Claims of Conscience, Cecil Evans, QHS 1996.

SOCIAL RESPONSIBILITY
Housing, Our Spiritual Concern, QSR&E, 1993.

Life and Work: some Quakers look at work and its place in our lives, QSR&E 1993.

Questions of Integrity, Committee for Truth and Integrity in Public Affairs, C&F 1993.

Beyond the Spirit of the Age, Jonathan Dale, QHS 1996.

MODERN QUAKERS
The Way Out is the Way In: a Quaker's pilgrimage, Damaris Parker-Rhodes, QHS 1985.

The Quaker Tapestry, Ormerod Greenwood, Impact Books 1990.

THEOLOGY & DOCTRINE
To Lima with Love: the response of the Religious Society of Friends in Great Britain to the World Council of Churches' document 'Baptism, Eucharist and Ministry', Committee on Christian Relationships, QHS 1987.

The End of Words: issues in contemporary Quaker theology, Rex Ambler, QHS 1994, rptd. 1995.

QUAKER ORGANISATIONS
Beyond Majority Rule: voteless decisions in the Religious Society of Friends, Michael Sheeran SJ, Philadelphia Yearly Meeting 1983.

These are some of a wide range of Quaker books which, together with other books on peace, social issues and religion in general, are available from:

THE
QUAKER BOOKSHOP,
Friends House, Euston Road,
London NW1 2BJ.

Tel: 0171-387-3601 ex: 2223.

INDEX

A